THE BIGGEST LOSER

FAMILY COOKBOOK

NBC

FAMILY COOKBOOK

Budget-Friendly Meals Your Whole Family Will Love

Chef Devin Alexander and *The Biggest Loser* Experts and Cast

with Melissa Roberson

Rodale books may be purchased for business or promotional use or for special sales. For information, please write to: Special Markets Department, Rodale Inc., 733 Third Avenue, New York, NY 10017

Printed in the United States of America
Rodale Inc. makes every effort to use acid-free ♾, recycled paper ♻.

Book design by Christina Gaugler
Illustration on page 9 by Judy Newhouse
Photo of Devin Alexander on page ix by benvil photography
Food photographs by Mitch Mandel. All other photos by NBC Universal Photo.

Library of Congress Cataloging-in-Publication Data

Alexander, Devin.
    The Biggest Loser family cookbook : budget-friendly meals your whole family will love / Devin Alexander and the Biggest Loser experts and cast with Melissa Roberson.
        p.   cm.
    Includes bibliographical references and index.
    ISBN-13 978–1–60529–783–5   paperback
    ISBN-10 1–60529–783–6   paperback
    1. Low budget cookery.   2. Reducing diets—Recipes.   3. Biggest loser (Television program)   I. Roberson, Melissa.   II. Biggest loser (Television program)   III. Title.
    TX652.A3844   2008
    641.5'52—dc22   2008040388

Distributed to the trade by Macmillan

8   10   9   paperback

Product Development and Direction: Chad Bennett, Dave Broome, Neysa Gordon, Mark Koops, Kim Niemi, Todd Nelson, J. D. Roth, Ben Silverman

NBCU, Reveille, 25/7 Productions, and 3Ball Productions would like to thank the many people who gave their time and energy to this project:

Jenna Alifante, Stephen Andrade, Dana Arnett, Sebastian Attie, Nancy N. Bailey, Jim Berra, Maria Bohe, Jen Busch, *The Biggest Loser* contestants, Jill Carmen, Scot Chastain, Ben Cohen, Jason Cooper, Dan Curran, Dr. Michael Dansinger, Beth Davey, Camilla Dhanak, Cori Diamond, Hayley Dickson, Lynn Donches, Milissa Douponce, Jenny Ellis, Kat Elmore, Cheryl Forberg, Kurt Ford, Jeff Gaspin, Christina Gaugler, Marc Graboff, Graham Greenlee, Libby Hansen, Bob Harper, Shelli Hill, Andrea Holt, Dr. Robert Huizenga, Jill Jarosz, Helen Jorda, Alex Katz, Allison Kaz, Connie Kempany, Loretta Kraft, Chris Krogermeier, Laura Kuhn, Beth Lamb, Jessica Lane, Melissa Leffler, Todd Lubin, Roni Lubliner, Alan Lundgren, Carole MacDonal, Rebecca Marks, Erin McGuigan, Joaquin Mesa, Jillian Michaels, Gregg Michaelson, John Miller, Ann Morteo, Steve Murphy, Kam Naderi, Julie Nugent, Blanca Oliviery, Bill Ostroff, Carole Panick, Joanne Park, Trae Patton, Jerry Petry, Craig Plestis, Chris Rhoads, Lee Rierson, Karen Rinaldi, Melissa Roberson, Beth Roberts, Jessica Roth, Joe Schlosser, Leslie Schwartz, Jennifer Scott, Robin Shallow, Carrie Simons, Hayley Sneiderman, Mitch Steele, Lee Straus, Kelia Tardiff, Deborah Thomas, Stacey Ward, Liza Whitcraft, Julie Will, Bob Wright, Yong Yam, Jeff Zucker

Contents

Introduction

When I started my own weight-loss journey back in the late '80s, dieting was lonely. I was one of the only kids in my high school who was overweight, let alone obese, and there was no one (at least to my knowledge) on TV giving weight-loss advice or talking about the subject at all. I struggled in silence, peaking somewhere over 190 pounds at 15 years old. I wondered if I'd ever even find a friend who would understand what my every day was like as an obese girl with a passionate spirit and a cute personality dying to emerge…if only given some glimmer of hope.

Fortunately, I found that hope in my late teens…in my kitchen, of all places. It was ironic, since that was also the location of some of my greatest struggles and many low moments when I just couldn't manage to tear myself away from the refrigerator, even though I desperately wanted to change. So you can imagine how ecstatic I am not only to have shifted my negative obsession with food into a fulfilling career, but also to be a part of *The Biggest Loser* community—a place where anyone struggling with weight can find the sort of friend that I so desperately needed.

Unlike the lonely battle I faced as a child, obesity has, regrettably, become a common issue for many

American families. Millions of parents are struggling to stay fit and ensure the lifelong heath of their children, all the while maintaining the family budget. A lot of people think that it's just too expensive to eat healthful, nutritious foods. And sure enough, grocery costs seem to be climbing higher each day. So what's a concerned, health-minded parent to do? I'm here to show that you can lose weight and feed your family delicious food without breaking the bank. This cookbook is full of wholesome recipes that can be easily adapted to fit into your budget. In the recipes themselves and throughout this book, you'll find cost-saving tips and recipe modifications from me and *The Biggest Loser* cast and experts to ensure that these meals won't break the bank.

A couple of years ago, when I agreed to write the first *Biggest Loser Cookbook*, I had no idea how powerfully it would impact my life and others. I've since been able to befriend a number of the contestants and work with even more. I've received thousands of letters from folks who are just like me or just like I was, who expressed shock at how tasty my healthy recipes are. I've since been called a "Kitchen Magician" and "America's Cool Food Chef" and have appeared on hundreds of TV spots, from the *Today* show to *The Biggest Loser*...and all because I have a deep love and passion for re-creating dishes that would otherwise be off-limits to those of us seeking to lose weight or maintain weight loss. *The Biggest Loser* has changed my life, and it is changing America.

I truly believe that it's easy to find freedom and enjoyment from food. You just need to learn some basic recipes and make family mealtime a priority in your household. Cooking is a valuable, lifelong skill, and getting your kids into the kitchen at a young age and encouraging them to participate in meal preparation will help them learn how to eat healthfully for many years to come. It sounds so simple, but I swear I would still be obese if I couldn't cook or if I hadn't ever heard that all you need to do to lose 10 pounds in a year (on average) is to cut 100 calories from your diet per day. Think about it: For a weekend breakfast with the family, you can rely on a local restaurant that serves overpriced veggie egg-white omelets, or you can flip to page 20 of this book and, in your own kitchen, make a Tex-Mex Mini-Frittata that is good enough to serve to guests (in case the in-laws decide to swing by for coffee). You can go out to lunch after the kids' soccer game and order a plain, baked chicken breast or head to page 118 to make Party Chicken Kebabs at a fraction of the price that are fun to eat and bursting with flavor. And you don't have to be a master chef.

Folks often ask me how I do it. They want to know why my healthy food tastes so good. There are two reasons. First of all, healthy food *is* my life. I live it. I breathe it. And I think it. As you'll see in the pages of this book, I don't just substitute fat-free this and fat-free that in obvious fashion or fill every dish with tofu and carrot sticks. Every recipe is carefully conceived, whether it is a quick throw-together for a weekday lunch on-the-go or a heartier family meal. And some of these recipes were actually cooked as many as 32 times to get the flavor profiles just as they should be—decadent, delicious, and not at all reminiscent of "diet food." And secondly, I am a culinary school graduate who is committed to putting cooking techniques to good use so that my recipes are no-brainers for you by the time they reach your family's kitchen.

You don't need to be a master chef or have trained for years to cook amazing dishes in your own kitchen. You just need to be stocked with an arsenal of fabulous recipes like the ones in *The Biggest Loser Cookbook*, and now *The Biggest Loser Family Cookbook*. As you flip through the pages and see vibrant images of foods like Grilled Chicken Smothered Nachos, Pizza Burgers, Baked Ziti, and even Chocolate Cherry Truffles, you'll quickly see that these recipes taste like the unhealthy, expensive restaurant foods that we crave, but they aren't. Believe me, you won't get food this healthy or this cost effective by ordering in or making a reservation. It's time to head to your own kitchen: It's where miracles do occur.

Chef Devin Alexander

Notes for the Chef, from the Chef

Though you won't need special equipment in order to make any of the dishes in this book, I would recommend that you consider purchasing the following three items.

Deli meat slicer: Most deli meats are absolutely packed with sodium—up to 800 or 900 milligrams (or more!) per 4-ounce serving. And the "lower sodium" varieties don't tend to be much better. If you're a big fan of deli sandwiches and are feeding a family, you may want to consider investing in a meat slicer. Over time, it will pay for itself, because it tends to be much less costly to buy turkey breasts and lean roasts that you can easily cook and slice than it is to purchase deli meats. Plus, you'll reduce your sodium intake, and you'll know the meat is fresh.

Kitchen scale: Though I've tried to provide cup measurements for all ingredient amounts, I'd highly recommend that you invest in a kitchen scale if you truly want to live a healthy lifestyle. Often people come to me unable to understand why they're not losing weight. In many cases, the problem is that they simply misjudge portion sizes. Check out *The Biggest Loser* Kitchen Scale by Taylor at retailers nationwide.

Olive oil sprayer: From where I stand, there's a big difference between olive oil spray and olive oil cooking spray. The first comes from a sprayer that you simply fill with your favorite olive oil (or extra-virgin olive oil). The latter (usually found with the oils in major grocery stores) is prefilled and most often contains propellants and other ingredients. I love to lightly mist extra-virgin olive oil spray directly onto my food at times (especially foods that are commonly fried), even after the food's been cooked, to give the dish an enhanced taste and texture. (You need very little oil.) You can't do that with olive oil cooking spray because of the added chemicals.

I've often been deemed "obsessively analytical" by reviewers of my recipes. And I am, which is how, I believe, I am able to make (and eat) seemingly decadent food and still maintain my 55-pound weight loss. When creating recipes, I'm very precise about every ingredient. Below are explanations of a few of my ingredient choices that might not otherwise be clear. I hope this will help you throughout this book and in your everyday healthy cooking.

Brown rice: I love short grain brown rice, which has a nuttier flavor and firmer texture than long grain rice. I'm not much of a fan of long grain, though medium grain is acceptable to me. Though long grain may be easier to find at the grocery store, it's worth a visit to your local health-food store to pick up short grain if you've never tried it.

Fresh herbs: Sure, fresh herbs take longer to chop. But they lend so much flavor to food, while adding few or no calories. If you don't know your basil from your rosemary or tarragon, take a trip to your local farmers' market (they're located pretty much everywhere these days!) and ask the growers for an education. Throwing a little fresh basil into a chopped salad or a bit of tarragon into an omelet can transform a blah meal into a seemingly gourmet feast with no harm to your hips or your heart. For a quick and easy way to chop up fresh herbs, check out *The Biggest Loser* Double Up Chopper and Blender by Taylor, available at retailers nationwide.

Fresh juices and garlic: Again, it takes a bit more effort, but I can't overemphasize how much better fresh-squeezed lemon, lime, and orange juices and freshly minced garlic taste compared with their bottled counterparts. Healthier dishes don't rely on fat, sugars, or salt for flavor, so if you cut corners on these other main sources of flavor, it's tough to enjoy healthful foods. For me, using the fresh stuff can be the difference between truly enjoying a dish and just "stomaching it." For a quick, easy way to juice fruit and more, check out *The Biggest Loser* Double Up Fruit and Vegetable Juice Extractor by Taylor, available at retailers nationwide.

Ground meats: If you have trouble finding extra-lean ground chicken, pork, veal, or even beef, don't despair. Butchers at most major grocery stores will grind meats fresh for you at no charge. Just take a package of chicken breast or a pork tenderloin to the counter and ask for assistance. Not only will you know the meat is fresh, but you may even save money over buying it preground. One more thing to note: Though many people substitute turkey for beef in meatballs, meat loaf, and other ground-meat dishes, this doesn't always work like a charm. The moisture content is different in the two, so a dish made with turkey doesn't necessarily turn out nearly as well if the original recipe was developed for beef. If you're just plain not a beef eater, I'd definitely consider substituting chicken (not turkey) for beef where needed, as the end result tends to more closely mimic the flavor and texture of beef.

Low-fat versus fat-free cheese: I much prefer low-fat cheese to fat-free cheese, but you may use either in these recipes. When cooking with low-fat or fat-free cheese, especially in recipes for pizza, tacos, or any other dish in which you want to achieve a gooey texture, always shred it finely. Not only will you need less quantity to get some cheese in every bite, but it will melt more uniformly and give you the cheesy factor you crave.

Low-fat versus fat-free mayonnaise: Though *The Biggest Loser* weight-loss plan allows the use of fat-free mayonnaise, I've used low-fat (one with 2 grams of fat per tablespoon) throughout the book. I haven't yet found a brand of fat-free that I didn't think had an aftertaste that would destroy the flavor of my dishes. If you've found a brand you like, I'd suggest adhering to the plan and using fat-free without exception. If you're like me and just plain don't enjoy the taste of fat-free, stick to the low-fat version. In the long run, if you enjoy the food, you're more likely to stick with a healthy eating plan long-term.

Low-carb versus low-fat tortillas: Though low-carb tortillas definitely tend to have more fiber and fewer carbs than low-fat ones do, they can also have much more sodium. If you're watching your sodium intake, always be sure to check the labels. Different brands of low-fat tortillas can vary widely in sodium content. Low-fat tortillas are also typically made with whole grains and natural ingredients. If you're making pizza crusts or cooking tortillas, I would definitely recommend that you opt for low-fat. Cooking low-carb tortillas may yield a chemical odor and taste when heated.

Slicing against the grain: To tenderize meat, you should always cut it against the grain. You can see lines running through steak and pork, and when you cut against these lines (perpendicular to them, not parallel), the knife will begin breaking down the fibers so your teeth don't have to. You also want to cut meat into thin slices—the more cuts your knife makes into a piece of meat, the more tender it will be.

Technique Notes

While the recipes in this book are easy enough for even the novice cook, there are a few things I'd like to clarify before you begin cooking.

"Chopped herbs" versus "herbs, chopped": When a recipe calls for "½ cup chopped herbs" (or chopped anything, for that matter), it means that you chop the ingredient, then measure out ½ cup. If it says, "½ cup herbs, chopped," you measure the herb whole, then chop it. This will yield significantly different amounts in the end, so it's worth noting.

Cooking meats: Whether you're pan-frying a chicken breast, cooking some strips of beef for a fajita, or grilling a burger, I can't emphasize enough how important it is to start with a well-heated skillet (a drop of water should sizzle when it touches the surface) before adding the meat. You also want to use a skillet that allows you to spread the food in a single layer. Cooking with a pan that's too small or over heat that's too low can cause the meat to virtually steam, preventing it from developing that wonderful browned coating that tastes and looks restaurant-perfect.

Ounce versus cup measures: Many of the recipes, especially those containing shredded cheese, list measurements in ounces and in cups. I strongly urge you to follow the ounce measurements if at all possible. Because the thickness of a shred, the density of a cheese, and so on contribute to how the cheese falls in a measuring cup, it's hard to make yields 100 percent accurate from kitchen to kitchen. But 4 ounces is 4 ounces whether it's shredded exceptionally finely or coarsely. The nutritional data is provided based on the ounce measurement. The cup measures are provided merely for convenience in case you don't own a scale.

"Trimmed chicken": When a recipe calls for 1 pound of trimmed chicken, it means that the quantity should be 1 pound *after* being trimmed. In other cookbooks, you may see the phrase "1 pound chicken, visible fat removed." That means you buy 1 pound of chicken, then remove any visible fat. I want you to be able to consume a full 4 ounces. So when you're purchasing, make sure the whole chicken weighs a bit over a pound.

The Weight of the Union

Let's face it: America has become a hefty nation. About two-thirds, or 66 percent, of us have been classified by health officials as overweight or obese. In the late '80s and early '90s, that statistic was 56 percent. In the late '70s, it was more like 47 percent. The numbers show a dramatic increase. Even more disturbing is the fact that about one-third of our children and teens are overweight or obese—*triple* the rate of their parents' and grandparents' generations. Doctors are diagnosing high blood pressure, high cholesterol, and type 2 diabetes in *elementary* school kids and, in some cases, predicting shorter life spans for them than their parents for the first time ever. What we eat today has an impact not only on our future, but on the future of our children. Trainers Bob Harper and Jillian Michaels on *The Biggest Loser* always shake their heads at the amount of fast food their contestants—and their families—are used to eating before they arrive at the ranch. "It's super-size this and super-size that," observes Harper, "with the result that portion sizes are out of control as well."

So how can you protect your family from our national health crisis? Two words: *family meals.* The demise of the once-hallowed ritual of family mealtime is emerging as a factor, say researchers, in this country's obesity epidemic. Studies indicate that dinnertime is the perfect opportunity to introduce healthy foods into your family's diet and to involve family members (that includes the kids!) in food choices, preparation, and cooking. But we're talking about more than just food. It's also a perfect time for family members to slow down and talk to each other. Parents might actually find out what's going on in their teenagers' lives! And when the dinner table is an enjoyable place—in terms of both food and environment—big strides can be made for the health of everyone sitting around it.

If family mealtime isn't already a part of your day, try to work it into your family's schedule so that it becomes a priority. Like soccer practice or day care, it will soon become an integral part of your day, and something you won't skip. If the kids are reluctant at first, start small. Gradually introducing change makes it easier for them to adjust. Start by filling everyone's drinking glass with water or skim milk instead of soda. Or turning off the TV during meals. And try to get your kids involved! Don't just put down a plate of food in front of them and say, "Eat it." Let them be involved in the shopping and meal preparation, and they might even try a few new vegetables.

We've witnessed firsthand the powerful influence of family on Season 6 of *The Biggest Loser.* Vicky and Brady Vilcan came to the ranch from Louisiana, worried about their weight but heartbroken about the example they were setting for their children, especially their daughter, who weighed 63 pounds at the age of 4. "I feel 100 percent responsible for my daughter. She's overweight, and I know it's because of me," said Vicky.

But after the Vilcans committed to a healthy way of life at the ranch, things changed. "Before my experience at *The Biggest Loser* ranch," said

significantly—not to mention the price of produce and other wholesome foods. A trip to the grocery store has become an exercise in sticker shock, while the low prices of many unhealthful, processed foods and fast foods has remained relatively stable.

Once *The Biggest Losers* leave the ranch and re-enter the real world, they're struggling with the same budgetary issues as the rest of us. But, as you'll see throughout this book, there's hope! "We have found that since we're not eating out like we used to, we actually have more money to spend on good, healthy food," says Stacey Capers, another Season 6 member. "So we've moved the 'dining out' part of our budget over to groceries. And we're always on the lookout for a good sale!" Cooking and eating at home not only ensures that you're eating healthy, nutritious foods—it also helps you save money.

Coleen Skeabeck of Season 6 adds, "For me, getting the best deal possible and not breaking the bank is so important. I shop at a local farmers' market to get the best prices on produce instead of buying it at the grocery store. As for the other groceries, I plan out what I'd like to eat for the next week or so and then buy only what I need instead of throwing a bunch of items in my cart. And although sometimes it takes a minute to flip through the ads, finding items you need that may be on sale really helps!"

Brady, "We often ate whenever and wherever we felt like. Ninety percent of the time, we ate at a restaurant or took home takeout. Now I spend a lot of time planning what to get from the grocery store to prepare at home. The first thing I do at mealtime is turn off the television. Mealtime is now family time, where we all sit together at the same time and share thoughts about the day."

Frustratingly, eating healthfully these days doesn't always come cheap. Even the cost of basic staples such as bread, milk, and eggs has climbed

So, how to prepare the best food at the best prices? To that end, Chef Devin Alexander has come up with more than 125 recipes specifically crafted to keep your wallet—and your family—healthy. These are true crowd-pleasing recipes that will get everyone in the kitchen and satisfy even the pickiest tastebuds. Since food prices vary across the country (groceries tend to be cheaper in the Midwest and more expensive in major metropolitan areas and on the East and West coasts), we've come up with recipe items that would fit a

weekly food budget of $175 to $215 for a family of four. For more information on the cost of groceries around the country, visit one of the Web sites listed in Resources on page 215.

There are no hard-and-fast rules when it comes to these recipes, and there's plenty of room to adjust for your family's budget and tastes. If a recipe calls for fresh vegetables but frozen are on sale at your local grocery store, go for what works best for you. Also, take advantage of your regional specialties. If you're in central Pennsylvania, for example, an area known for its farms and dairy cattle, milk and produce will be cheaper. On the West Coast, you may find better deals on salmon than the rest of us. And if you live in Florida, you'll have much cheaper access to citrus fruits than folks elsewhere in the country. It all depends on where the product originates and what your family likes. For more information about what's in season where you live, check out the Web sites listed in Resources on page 215.

Put yourself in control. The idea here is to have fun, eat well, and enjoy your family—all without going broke!

Watch Your Wallet

You'll find budget shopping tips throughout this book, but here are a few hard-core essentials that will get you started on the right foot.

- Make a list and don't leave home without it! Plan your meals in advance, itemize what you need, and stick to it. That way you can avoid the potato chip aisle.

- Buy less-expensive store brands or try warehouse or discount stores.

- Stock up on sale items that are nonperishable, such as canned goods.

- Don't forget the lowly bean! It offers great nutrition at a bargain price.

- Shop the outer aisles of the grocery store. That's where you'll find fresh fruits and vegetables, lean proteins, and fat-free dairy products. The inner aisles contain most of the processed, less healthy stuff.

- Always check the unit pricing on an item, not just the total price, to make sure you're getting the best deal. The best savings aren't always on the largest quantity.

- Study the store circulars carefully to make sure you're getting a real discount. Sometimes manufacturers pay to have an item included in the circular, so compare weekly specials to the non-"special" brands to find the best deal.

- Don't always buy the items on display at eye level. Cheaper items are usually on the bottom shelf, and not at the ends of aisles.

- If you enjoy cooking with fresh herbs, investing in a small window box filled with your favorites is a good option. You'll always have fresh herbs at your fingertips. To keep herbs that grow quickly from going to seed, clip and freeze as needed. Here's how: Wash and finely chop the herbs, then fill the sections of an ice cube tray about halfway with the herb pieces. Cover the herbs with water, pop the tray in the freezer, and freeze until solid. Once cubes are formed, transfer your "herb ice cubes" to an airtight container and store it in the freezer. Add the cubes while preparing moist recipes such as hot soups, stews, and sauces.

2

Nutrition Overview

efore each season of *The Biggest Loser* begins to film, the new cast members report to the ranch and sit down for an intensive one-on-one with the show's nutritionist, Cheryl Forberg, RD. Forberg works with the contestants individually to review their eating habits and assess their dietary needs. Do they eat breakfast? Do they salt their food? How much dairy do they consume daily? What about fresh fruits and vegetables? How much fast food do they typically eat in a week? Forberg puts each person through a thorough list of questions.

Every season, says Forberg, there are a few contestants who eat *lots* of fast food (some as much as 90 percent of their diet!), skip breakfast, drink many glasses of sugar-laden soda daily, and *might* get as many servings of fruits and vegetables in an entire week as they should be eating each day.

As they prepare to enter the world of the ranch and cook from the well-stocked *Biggest Loser* kitchen, these contestants are about to make some big adjustments. Among them:

- They're probably going to eat more often throughout the day than they ever have before: three meals and two snacks, all with a healthy punch of protein and fresh fruit and vegetables.

- They're going to eat breakfast within half an hour of waking up (to get their bodies revved up for the day's first workout).

- They're going to drink lots of water, not only to hydrate, says Forberg, but to keep those nutrients and vitamins traveling throughout their bodies for an extra energy boost.

- They're going to meet—and embrace—a whole new world of fresh fruits and vegetables, often some they've never tasted before, such as spaghetti squash, a ranch kitchen staple. (For a video on how Season 5 winner Ali Vincent prepares spaghetti squash, go to biggestloserclub.com/families.)

Whether you're at the ranch or in your own home, *The Biggest Loser* eating plan is sensible, healthy, and flexible—and can be maintained for the rest of your life. This is a lifestyle, not a diet. What makes it work are the principles of calorie control, carbohydrate modification, fat-intake reduction, and lean protein intake (which helps control hunger). You get to eat three meals and two snacks each day, so you never feel hungry or deprived. The program encourages you to eat an array of fresh, wholesome foods that vary in color and texture. Natural, unprocessed foods are an important part of the program. They tend to have fewer calories than processed foods and also contain more fiber, which keeps hunger at bay longer.

One important lesson all contestants on the show learn: Squeeze as many nutrients as possible into your daily allotted calories.

Calories Are Your Friends

Calories often take a beating in the world of weight loss. We hate to count them, and we think we're not going to be given enough of them to stay satisfied. But if you pick your calories wisely, as the delicious foods in this plan allow you to do, you'll have plenty to go around, and you'll love every single one!

If you were put on the spot and asked to give a simple definition of a calorie, what would you say? Hopefully, something like: **A calorie is the unit of measurement of how much energy a food gives your body after you eat it.** In other words, you need calories to live, and if they're the right kind of calories, you live better. The catch is, if you eat more calories than you burn, you'll gain

THE 4-3-2-1 BIGGEST LOSER PYRAMID

The Extras
200 calories daily

Whole grains
2 servings daily

Protien Foods
3 servings daily

Fruits and Vegetables
At least 4 servings daily

weight, whether the calories come from healthful, natural foods or unhealthful, processed ones.

Here's the simple math on how many calories you need to lose weight:

**Your present weight × 7 =
Your daily calorie needs for weight loss**

If you weigh more than 300 pounds, start by eating 2,100 calories a day. If you weigh less than 150 pounds, plan to eat around 1,050 calories a day.

Best Foods for Best Results

For an easy visual reference as to how you should eat on a daily basis, let's go to the 4-3-2-1 *Biggest Loser* Pyramid.

4: The bottom, or widest, tier represents the **fruits and vegetables** in your diet. You should eat **at least 4 servings daily.**

3: The next tier up represents **protein foods,** of which you should have **3 servings daily.**

2: The next tier is for **whole grains,** of which you should have **2 servings daily.**

1: The top tier is for **extras**, of which you're allowed up to **200 calories daily**.

A Closer Look: Fruits and Vegetables

Servings: 4 daily, minimum

At least half of your servings in this group should be from vegetables, the other half from fruits. Don't have more fruit servings than vegetable servings. Try eating a vegetable salad most days of the week and try to eat at least one raw fruit and one raw vegetable each day.

Fruit

Serving sizes: 1 cup, 1 medium piece, or 8 ounces

Try these: Apple, apricot, banana, blackberries, blueberries, cherries, cranberries, grapefruit, grapes, guava, kiwifruit, mango, melon (all varieties), nectarine, orange, papaya, peach, pear, persimmon, pineapple, plum, pomegranate, raspberries, rhubarb, strawberries, tangerine, watermelon

Not these: Dried fruits (not as filling as raw, highly caloric, and often full of fruit sugar and additives), fruit juices (missing the fiber of whole fruit)

Vegetables

Serving sizes: 1 cup or 8 ounces

Try these: Artichoke, asparagus, bamboo shoots, beans (green, yellow), beet greens, beets, bell peppers, broccoli, brussels sprouts, cabbage, carrots, cauliflower, celery, collard greens, cucumbers, eggplant, kale, kohlrabi, leeks, lettuce (all varieties), mushrooms, mustard greens, okra, onions, palm hearts, parsley, peas, peppers (all varieties), radishes, shallots, spinach, sprouts, summer squash, Swiss chard, tomatillos, tomatoes, turnip greens, turnips, water chestnuts, watercress, zucchini

Try these in moderation: Pumpkin, sweet potatoes, winter squash, yams (starchy vegetables that are higher in calories and carbs; have just a few servings of them a week)

Not these: White potatoes (which Forberg says can send blood sugar soaring and may increase food cravings)

A Closer Look: Protein

Servings: 3 daily

For flexibility, choose from three different types of protein: animal, vegetarian, and low-fat and fat-free dairy. Protein is best eaten in smaller quantities at a time so your body can use it throughout the day. Aim to eat a serving of protein at each meal and half a serving with each snack.

Animal Protein

Serving sizes: 1 cup or 8 ounces

Try these: Any type of beef, pork, or veal

labeled 95 percent lean; egg whites; fish (any type; try to choose fish that's rich in the heart-protective fats called omega-3 fatty acids, such as salmon, herring, trout, and tuna); shellfish, such as crab, shrimp, and clams; white-meat chicken; white-meat turkey

Try these in moderation: Red meats, such as beef and steak. Limit servings to two a week, since red meats tend to be high in saturated fat.

Not these: Processed or smoked meats, such as bologna, hot dogs, salami, sausages, and so forth. These meats are generally high in fat and may contain sodium nitrites, which react with the food in your stomach to form highly carcinogenic (potentially cancer-causing) compounds.

Vegetarian Protein

Serving sizes: 1 cup or 8 ounces

Try these: Beans and legumes (black beans, broad beans, chickpeas, edamame, great northern beans, kidney beans, lentils, lima beans, navy beans, pinto beans, split peas, white beans, and so forth); miso, soybeans, and other natural soy products (not the powders or pills); tempeh; tofu; soy milk

Low-Fat Dairy Protein

Serving sizes: 1 cup or 8 ounces

Try these: Buttermilk; fat-free yogurt (no sugar added); low-fat (1 percent) or skim (fat-free) milk; reduced-fat cottage cheese

Try these in moderation: Low-fat frozen yogurt, low-fat ice cream, low-fat or part-skim cheeses, low-fat sour cream; nonfat whipped topping

Not these: Cream cheese, full-fat cheeses, full-fat sour cream, ice cream, whipped cream, whole milk

A Closer Look: Whole Grains

Servings: 2 daily

Whole grains undergo very little processing, so they retain nutrients. Choose rolled oats over instant, and choose breads that have 2 or more grams of fiber per serving. Opt for low-carb, high-fiber cereals that have at least 5 grams of fiber per serving and less than 5 grams of sugars per serving.

Breads

Serving sizes: 2 slices bread, preferably "light"; 1 whole grain bun or roll; 2 light Wasa flatbreads; 1 whole wheat flour tortilla

Try these: Ezekiel bread; high-fiber bread (choose brands with around 45 calories per slice); Wasa bread; whole grain bread; whole wheat buns; whole wheat dinner rolls; whole wheat pitas; whole wheat tortillas and low-carb wraps

Not these: "White stuff," such as white bread and white pasta

Cereals, Grains, and Pasta

Serving size: 1 cup cooked

Try these: Barley, brown rice, bulgur, corn grits, couscous, cream of rice, cream of wheat, millet, oat bran, quinoa, rolled oats, whole wheat cereal (such as All-Bran, Fiber One, or Kashi GoLean), whole wheat pasta, wild rice

Not these: Instant oats, most ready-to-eat breakfast cereals, white rice

A Closer Look: Extras

You're allotted 200 extra calories a day in addition to those you take in from the foods above. The goal here is to spend the remainder of your calorie budget on healthy choices and not squander it on nutritionally bankrupt foods such as candy or sweets. Make sensible, healthy choices from among the following foods and condiments.

Fats, Oils, and Spreads

Try these: Canola oil, flaxseed oil, olive oil, or walnut oil; reduced-fat or fat-free salad dressings and mayonnaise; reduced-fat peanut butter and nut butters

Not these: Butter or margarine, full-fat dressings, full-fat nut butters, peanut oil, vegetable oil, vegetable shortening

Desserts and Sweets

Try these: Reduced-calorie jams, jellies, and syrups; sugar-free, fat-free puddings and gelatins; sugar-free, fat-free whipped topping; sugar-free Popsicles and Fudgsicles

Not these: Cakes, candy, cookies, doughnuts, pastries, pies

Condiments and Sauces

Try these: Chili sauce, cocktail sauce, horseradish, low-calorie barbecue sauce, low-calorie ketchup, low-sodium soy sauce, mustard, picante sauce, reduced-sodium broths or bouillons, salsa, steak sauce, Tabasco sauce, tomato paste, tomato sauce, Worcestershire sauce

Not these: Cheese- or cream-based sauces, honey mustard, sweet and sour sauce, teriyaki sauce

Spices and Herbs

Try these: Basil, cinnamon, chili pepper, cumin, curry powder, dill, garlic, ginger, lavender, mint, nutmeg, onions, oregano, paprika, parsley, rosemary, saffron, sage, tarragon, thyme, turmeric

Extras in Moderation

Try these: Artificial sweeteners, avocado, nuts and seeds, olives, pickles (unsweetened varieties)

Not these: Animal fats (found in egg yolks,

full-fat dairy products, and meat products), trans fats (found in margarine and processed foods that feature "hydrogenated" or "partially hydrogenated" oils in the list of ingredients)

Water, Water

Yep, for weight loss, the drink of choice is water, and plenty of it—6 to 8 cups a day. If you need an extra inducement, try jazzing up a pitcher of water with citrus fruits or cucumber, or herbs such as mint or basil.

Other beverages you may drink in moderation and in addition to water are . . .

- No-calorie flavored water
- Coffee or tea (caffeinated or decaffeinated)
- Diet sodas (limit these to one or two a day)
- Herbal teas

What about Alcohol?

Never say never. Alcohol is not a total no-no on *The Biggest Loser* diet. After all, you can build it into your calorie budget. A 12-ounce regular beer contains about 150 calories, a 5-ounce glass of wine packs about 100 calories, and 1.5 ounces of 80-proof distilled spirits has about 100 calories. But keep in mind that when you drink, your inhibitions can become lowered, and you might be tempted to make poor food choices. An occasional drink is okay. But be careful, especially in the early stages of your new, healthy eating program.

What If You Slip?

Okay, so you went out on the town and had two more margaritas than you intended or an extra slice of birthday cake or scoop of ice cream. Whatever. A slip is a slip, not a recipe for disaster. This is what you do: You get up again the next day and start fresh. You get back on the program. Many a *Biggest Loser* has left the ranch and realized that a slip doesn't have to turn into a free fall. As you gain strength from healthy eating day by day, you'll realize that you do have what it takes to become a *Biggest Loser*—and stay one.

3

Breakfast: The Morning Battle

Breakfast. If it were a person, it might have the biggest inferiority complex in the world. People skip it, are repulsed by it, skimp on it, or acquire it from about the worst possible source: fast-food drive-throughs. Then there's the timing issue: Breakfast has to compete with the daily morning chaos of getting the family up, dressed, organized, and out the door to school or work. Oh, and somebody please walk the dog.

But let's face facts: Studies show that if you don't eat a healthy, nutritious breakfast, you're more likely to overeat later in the day. You're also more likely to space out and have difficulty concentrating in the morning, whether it's at school or at work. Bottom line: If you don't jumpstart your brain and metabolism with a healthy breakfast, you're not getting your day off to a great start. Trainer Jillian Michaels drills breakfast into her contestants on the show. She wants them up and eating within half an hour so they'll be ready for their morning workout.

Many *Biggest Loser* cast members come to the ranch having to rethink their relationship with the first meal of the day. Coleen Skeabeck, of Season 6, says, "Breakfast and I were sort of in a fight before *The Biggest Loser.* I'd eat a bowl of sugary cereal while getting ready for work, and then when I got to work, I'd pick up a Danish and coffee. (Yes, I ate breakfast *twice.*)"

Season 6 contestant Ed Brantley, a catering chef, was so focused on working in the morning that he didn't eat breakfast until 2 p.m., many hours after he'd woken up. And sometimes that first meal was a couple of fast-food cheeseburgers. *Biggest Loser* Tom Desrochers Sr. ate breakfast, all right— sometimes a 32-ounce diet soda and some pickles.

When it comes to breakfast, rule number one is: Eat it every day, no skipping. If you're not used to eating something within an hour of waking, you'll have to teach your body to re-cue its hunger signals, says *Biggest Loser* nutritionist Cheryl Forberg, RD. Try starting small and eating something simple, such as a bowl of fruit or a slice of whole grain toast. Soon you'll begin to wake up hungry and ready for a full breakfast every day.

As you become a breakfast pro, you'll learn about a wide variety of delicious foods that get your body and mind going, such as the ones featured in these recipes. As Coleen Skeabeck attests, she's revised her breakfast (and just one daily!) to look something like this: "I make myself egg whites, turkey bacon, and a piece of whole grain toast and fruit, *or* a bowl of high-fiber, high-protein cereal (like Kashi GoLean) with skim milk and sliced strawberries."

Most Important, Breakfast for Kids

For kids and teens, breakfast is especially important. Not only does regularly eating breakfast help them stay fit and healthy, it also affects their performance in school. According to a 2005 article published in the *Journal of the American Dietetic Association,* researchers who studied children and adolescents found a connection between eating breakfast regularly and maintaining a healthy weight. The kids and teens who ate breakfast also appeared to have higher test scores, better grades, and better school attendance.

Not only that, but when kids learn to eat a healthy breakfast, their chances of turning into healthy adults vastly improve. Many of *The Biggest Loser* cast members come to the ranch vowing to turn around not only their health, but the health of their families. They're ready to become role models for their kids. And it all starts with breakfast.

Breakfasts for the Whole Family

BROCCOLI AND CHEDDAR MINI-FRITTATAS

These quick and easy miniature frittatas make an elegant brunch offering. Just note that they tend to puff up quite a bit in the oven. After resting out of the oven, they should deflate a little—but they'll still look great on the plate and taste delicious!

Olive oil spray

1 cup chopped steamed broccoli

2 cups egg substitute

2 ounces (1 cup) finely shredded Cabot's 75% Light Cheddar Cheese, or your favorite low-fat Cheddar

Preheat the oven to 350°F. Lightly mist 8 cups of a nonstick standard muffin tin with the olive oil spray.

Divide the broccoli evenly among the cups (2 tablespoons in each). Then divide the egg substitute evenly among the cups (¼ cup in each). Bake the frittatas for 7 to 9 minutes, or until almost set.

Sprinkle the cheese evenly over the tops of the frittatas. Bake for 8 to 10 minutes longer, or until the egg is no longer runny and the cheese is melted. Transfer the muffin tin to a cooling rack and allow the frittatas to rest for 2 minutes before serving.

Makes 4 (2-frittata) servings

Per serving: **102 calories, 18 g protein, 4 g carbohydrates, 2 g fat (less than 1 g saturated), 5 mg cholesterol, 1 g fiber, 362 mg sodium**

Ali Vincent, Season 5 Winner

I always eat within half an hour of waking up to jump-start my metabolism. Then I eat every 3 to 4 hours, be it a meal or a snack. I think this is just as important for me as exercise.

WILD WEST FRITTATA

If you can't find an affordable ham steak in the cold meat section, you can always try the deli case. Just ask for one slice of extra-lean ham that is about ¼" thick. It's likely to be just about what you need.

Olive oil spray

¾ cup chopped sweet onion

½ cup chopped green bell pepper

4 ounces 97% or 98% lean ham steak, cut into ¼" cubes

Salt, to taste

Ground black pepper, to taste

2 cups egg substitute

2 ounces (1 cup) finely shredded light Swiss cheese

Preheat the broiler.

Place a medium broiler-safe nonstick skillet over medium heat. Lightly mist the skillet with the olive oil spray. Add the onion, bell pepper, and ham and cook for 5 to 7 minutes, or until the onion and pepper are softened but not browned. Season with salt and pepper (keep in mind that you will be adding ham and cheese, so you won't need much salt).

Turn the heat to medium-high and pour the egg substitute into the pan. Stir the veggies and ham in the eggs until they are evenly distributed and the eggs are slightly scrambled, 1 to 2 minutes. Reduce the heat to medium. Continue to cook, continuously sliding a spatula all around the sides of the frittata as far into the bottom as possible to loosen and gently lift the eggs slightly from the pan to prevent sticking, until the frittata is almost set but still runny on top, 4 to 6 minutes.

Remove the pan from the heat and sprinkle the cheese evenly over the top. Transfer the skillet to the oven and broil for 1 to 3 minutes, or until the cheese is melted and the egg is completely set. Cut the frittata into four equal wedges and serve.

Makes 4 servings

Per serving: 142 calories, 22 g protein, 7 g carbohydrates, 2 g fat (2 g saturated), 13 mg cholesterol, less than 1 g fiber, 621 mg sodium

TEX-MEX MINI-FRITTATAS

Mild green chiles provide subtle South-of-the-border flair to these easy frittatas. They're great for entertaining or just enjoying with your family.

Olive oil spray

2 cups egg substitute

2 ounces (1 cup) finely shredded Cabot's 75% Light Cheddar Cheese, or your favorite low-fat Cheddar

¼ cup drained canned diced green chiles

Preheat the oven to 350°F. Lightly mist 8 cups of a nonstick standard muffin tin with the olive oil spray.

Divide the egg substitute evenly among the muffin cups (¼ cup in each). Bake for 7 to 9 minutes, or until almost set.

In a small mixing bowl, mix the cheese and chiles. Sprinkle the mixture evenly over the tops of the frittatas. Bake for 8 to 10 minutes longer, or until the egg is no longer runny and the cheese is melted. Transfer the muffin tin to a cooling rack and allow the frittatas to rest for 2 minutes before serving.

Makes 4 (2-frittata) servings

Per serving: 94 calories, 17 g protein, 3 g carbohydrates, 1 g fat (less than 1 g saturated), 5 mg cholesterol, less than 1 g fiber, 386 mg sodium

Amy and Phillip Parham, Season 6

Our oldest son always ate sugary cereals for breakfast, but now he is eating turkey bacon and eggs or oatmeal with us. Our sons have even learned how to make scrambled eggs!

FAMILY FAVORITE BREAKFAST SCRAMBLE

Scrambles are a super-easy way to start your day. Although I'm generally not a fan of cooking in the microwave, I find it can be a good way to scramble egg whites. Just be sure to continually push the cooked egg toward the middle of the bowl while microwaving and they'll be perfectly fluffy and evenly cooked.

Olive oil spray

4 slices extra-lean turkey bacon, chopped

1 cup finely chopped sweet onion

2 teaspoons freshly minced garlic

16 large egg whites

3 cups loosely packed spinach leaves, stems removed

Salt, to taste

Ground black pepper, to taste

Place a large nonstick skillet over medium-high heat. Lightly mist the pan with the olive oil spray. Add the bacon, onion, and garlic and cook, stirring frequently, for 3 to 5 minutes, or until the onion is tender and the bacon is golden brown.

Meanwhile, mist a large shallow microwave-safe bowl with the spray. Add the egg whites and cover the bowl with microwave-safe plastic wrap. Microwave on high for 1½ minutes. Uncover the bowl and, using a fork, push the cooked portions of the whites from the outside toward the middle of the bowl, letting the runny, uncooked parts run to the outer edge. Re-cover the bowl and microwave in 30-second intervals until the whites are just a bit runny on top. Uncover, then using a fork, stir the whites to break into large "scrambled" pieces. By the time you scramble and stir them, the residual heat should have cooked away the runniness. If they are still undercooked, re-cover and continue cooking in 10-second intervals until just done (be careful not to overcook).

Add the scrambled egg whites and the spinach to the bacon mixture and stir well to wilt the spinach slightly and incorporate the egg whites. Season with salt and pepper. Divide the scramble among 4 plates and serve.

Makes 4 servings

Per serving: 109 calories, 19 g protein, 6 g carbohydrates, less than 1 g fat (trace saturated), 10 mg cholesterol, 1 g fiber, 381 mg sodium

SMOKED SAUSAGE BREAKFAST SCRAMBLE

Scrambles are an ideal breakfast for weight loss or maintenance because you can eat such a large portion for so few calories—and they're packed with protein. Here, I love the smoky sausage flavor with the cool freshness of the uncooked tomatoes. It's a breakfast that feels indulgent without actually doing damage.

Olive oil spray

4 ounces extra-lean fully cooked smoked turkey sausage or kielbasa (5 grams fat or less per 2-ounce serving), diced

1 cup finely chopped sweet onion

2 teaspoons freshly minced garlic

16 large egg whites

1 cup chopped seeded tomato

Salt, to taste

Ground black pepper, to taste

Place a large nonstick skillet over medium-high heat. Lightly mist the skillet with the olive oil spray. Add the sausage or kielbasa, onion, and garlic and cook, stirring frequently, for 3 to 5 minutes, or until the sausage is heated through and the onion is tender but not browned.

Meanwhile, spray a large, shallow microwave-safe bowl with the spray. Add the egg whites and cover the bowl with microwave-safe plastic wrap. Microwave on high for 1½ minutes. Uncover the bowl and, using a fork, push the cooked portions of the whites into the middle of the bowl, letting the runny, uncooked parts run toward the outer edge. Re-cover the bowl and microwave in 30-second intervals until the egg whites are just a bit runny on top. Uncover, then using a fork, stir the whites to break into large "scrambled" pieces. By the time you scramble and stir them, the residual heat should have cooked away the runniness. If they are still undercooked, re-cover and continue cooking in 10-second intervals until just done (be careful not to overcook).

Add the scrambled egg whites and the tomato to the sausage mixture. Stir well to slightly warm the tomatoes and incorporate the egg whites. Season with salt and pepper. Divide among 4 plates and serve.

Makes 4 servings

Per serving: 141 calories, 19 g protein, 8 g carbohydrates, 3 g fat (1 g saturated), 20 mg cholesterol, 1 g fiber, 471 mg sodium

BREAKFAST (SWEET) POTATOES

If you and your family are fans of hashed browns from the local breakfast dive, you'll love this more realistic and scrumptious version. If you have a really good nonstick baking sheet, you can skip the parchment, though using it will save you cleanup time and guarantee no sticking.

1 pound sweet potatoes, peeled and cut into ½" cubes

½ cup chopped green bell pepper

¾ cup chopped sweet onion

1½ teaspoons freshly minced garlic

1½ teaspoons extra-virgin olive oil

¼ teaspoon paprika

⅛ teaspoon salt, plus more to taste

Ground black pepper, to taste

Ground red pepper, to taste

Preheat the oven to 400°F. Line a large baking sheet with parchment paper.

In a medium glass or plastic mixing bowl, combine the sweet potatoes, bell pepper, onion, garlic, olive oil, paprika, and ⅛ teaspoon salt and toss well to combine. Transfer to the prepared baking sheet and arrange in a single layer.

Bake for 20 minutes. Turn the potato pieces with a spatula and bake 20 to 25 minutes longer, or until the potatoes are tender and the onion and pepper are lightly browned. Season with additional salt and black pepper and red pepper. Serve immediately.

Makes 4 servings

Per serving: 125 calories, 2 g protein, 25 g carbohydrates, 2 g fat (trace saturated), 0 mg cholesterol, 4 g fiber, 133 mg sodium

Curtis Bray, Season 5

Create meals around your *favorite* vegetables. If you hate squash, for example, don't cook it or force yourself to eat it. There is nothing worse then resenting the choice to eat healthy.

BANANA CREAM OF WHEAT

If you're looking for a hearty breakfast for a cold winter morning, you've flipped to the right page. In fact, the servings are so big and filling, half a serving might be enough if you're simply looking for a warm, satisfying breakfast. If you're hungry, a full serving is perfect.

4 cups water

⅛ teaspoon salt

¾ cup uncooked original (2½-minute) Cream of Wheat

1 cup mashed, ripe banana (about 2 small bananas)

1 teaspoon ground cinnamon

8 packets (.035 ounce each) sugar substitute (such as Splenda)

4 tablespoons crunchy high-fiber, low-sugar cereal (such as Grape-Nuts)

Place the water and salt in a medium nonstick saucepan and bring to a boil. Add the Cream of Wheat, stirring constantly until well blended. Return to a boil and reduce the heat to low. Simmer, stirring constantly, for 2 to 3 minutes, or until thickened. Remove from the heat and add the banana, cinnamon, and sugar substitute. Stir until well combined.

Divide among 4 serving bowls. Sprinkle 1 tablespoon of the crunchy cereal over each and serve.

Makes 4 servings

Per serving: 204 calories, 4 g protein, 46 g carbohydrates, trace fat (trace saturated), 0 mg cholesterol, 4 g fiber, 123 mg sodium

Budget Tips from The Biggest Loser

Instead of stopping by your local latte shop every morning, brew your own coffee at home and pour it into a reusable mug to take on-the-go. You'll be less tempted to add the whipped cream or caramel, and you'll save big bucks.

CANTALOUPE WEDGES

Fiber-enriched yogurt is a great way to add even more fiber to this meal if you have a bit of extra money in your budget or you find the yogurt on sale. Fiber One offers a number of flavored yogurts—each packs 5 grams of fiber into each 4-ounce container. It will add 2 grams of fiber per serving to this refreshing breakfast.

1 medium ripe cantaloupe

1 (6-ounce) container fat-free, sugar-free vanilla yogurt

1 cup fresh blueberries

On a large cutting board with a very sharp knife, cut the cantaloupe in half across the stem end. Scoop out the seeds, then cut each half in half, creating 4 wedges. Place the wedges on a serving plate and top each with one-fourth of the yogurt (about 2 tablespoons) and ¼ cup blueberries. Serve immediately.

Makes 4 servings

Per serving: 90 calories, 3 g protein, 21 g carbohydrates, trace fat (trace saturated), less than 1 mg cholesterol, 2 g fiber, 47 mg sodium

From the Experts

Watch for those little sale signs in your grocery store. Often they'll advertise special prices for the purchase of two items at a lower price or two for the price of one. That's great if you need two items, but if not, know that you usually get the same savings by buying just one of those special items.

—Louise Massey, RD, nutrition expert
for BiggestLoserClub.com

Individual, On-the-Go Breakfasts

BACON, EGG, AND CHEESE BREAKFAST SANDWICH

If you time it so that the egg and the muffin are done at the same time, the heat between them will perfectly melt the cheese for this drippy sandwich that easily rivals your favorite fast food version.

1 strip extra-lean turkey bacon, cut in half crosswise

Olive oil spray

1 large egg white

1 light multigrain or whole wheat English muffin (8 grams fiber per muffin; I used Thomas') , toasted

1 (¾-ounce) slice fat-free yellow American cheese

Place a small nonstick skillet over medium-high heat and add the bacon. Cook for 2 to 3 minutes per side, or until crisp. Remove from the pan and cover to keep warm.

Spray a 3½" or 4" microwave-safe bowl with the olive oil spray and add the egg white. Microwave for 30 seconds. Continue microwaving in 15-second intervals until it is just set completely.

Assemble the sandwich by placing the bottom half of the warm English muffin, inside up, on a plate. Top with the cheese, the egg, then the bacon. Add the English muffin top and serve.

Makes 1 serving

Per serving: 183 calories, 17 g protein, 25 g carbohydrates, 5 g fat (2 g saturated), 22 mg cholesterol, 8 g fiber, 625 mg sodium

Budget Tips from The Biggest Loser

Egg substitute and egg white-only products can be a lot more expensive than eggs. Save money by buying a dozen eggs, instead, and using only the whites. If you have a friend or neighbor who can make use of the yolks—all the better!

SPINACH, EGG, AND CHEESE BREAKFAST WRAP

Wraps are a quick and easy way to get plenty of nutrients any time of the day—if you fill them with smart choices. But be careful when choosing your tortilla. Many varieties are loaded with tons of sodium and don't taste any better than healthier versions.

1 (7½") low-carb, whole wheat or multigrain tortilla

Olive oil spray

3 egg whites

1 ounce (½ cup) finely shredded Cabot's 75% Light Cheddar Cheese

¼ cup fresh spinach leaves, stems removed

Place a small nonstick skillet over medium-high heat and add the tortilla (no need to add any fat). Heat the tortilla until just warm, about 30 seconds per side after the pan is heated.

Spray a small microwave-safe bowl with the olive oil spray and add the egg whites. Microwave on low for 30 seconds. Continue microwaving in 30-second intervals until the whites are just a bit runny on top. Stir with a fork, breaking the whites into large pieces. By the time you "scramble" and stir them, the residual heat should have cooked away the runniness. If they are still undercooked, cook in 10-second intervals until just done.

Place the warmed tortilla on a plate. Starting at the top, sprinkle the cheese in a 3" strip down the center to about 2" from the bottom. Top with half of the egg whites, the spinach leaves, then the remaining whites. Fold up the bottom so that the bare part is over the filling. Fold the sides into the center over the egg and serve.

Makes 1 serving

Per serving: 214 calories, 27 g protein, 15 g carbohydrates, 5 g fat (2 g saturated), 10 mg cholesterol, 8 g fiber, 493 mg sodium

Jay Kruger, Season 5

Always eat a healthy breakfast! I find that a meal that includes eggs or egg whites with whole grains makes a very satisfying morning meal.

HAM AND ASPARAGUS OMELET

When I first looked at the nutritional information for this omelet, I thought it had to be a mistake—1 gram of fat in a ham omelet? But then I realized there was no mistake: Even when using 97% lean ham, you're only using an ounce—which is plenty—that has less than 1 gram fat. If you don't mind a bit more fat, make the omelet extra special by adding 1 ounce of Cabot's 75% Light Cheddar Cheese. It'll add 61 calories and 2.5 grams fat.

Olive oil spray

1 ounce 97% or 98% lean ham steak cut into small cubes (or ham slices cut into strips)

⅓ cup chopped asparagus spears

¼ cup finely chopped sweet onion

½ teaspoon freshly minced garlic

4 large egg whites

Salt, to taste

Ground black pepper, to taste

Place a small nonstick skillet over medium-high heat. Lightly mist the pan with the olive oil spray. Add the ham, asparagus, onion, and garlic and cook, stirring frequently, for 3 to 5 minutes, or until the asparagus is crisp-tender and the onion is tender. Remove the pan from the heat and cover to keep warm.

In a medium bowl, whisk the egg whites with a fork until they bubble lightly. Season with salt and pepper.

Place a small nonstick skillet over medium heat. Lightly mist the pan with the spray. Add the egg whites and cook, lifting the edges with a spatula as they start to set and tipping the pan to allow the uncooked whites to run underneath, for 4 to 6 minutes, or until almost set. Flip the omelet. Sprinkle the ham mixture over half of the omelet. Flip the bare half over the filled half and transfer to a serving plate. Serve immediately.

Makes 1 serving

Per serving: **125 calories, 21 g protein, 7 g carbohydrates, 1 g fat (less than 1 g saturated), 8 mg cholesterol, 1 g fiber, 527 mg sodium**

MUSHROOM-SWISS OMELET

This omelet is great with any variety of mushroom. We suggest button mushrooms as they tend to be the least expensive. But if portobellos are on sale, definitely indulge.

Olive oil spray

½ cup sliced button mushrooms

1 teaspoon freshly minced garlic

Salt, to taste

Ground black pepper, to taste

4 large egg whites

¾ ounce (⅓ cup) finely shredded or thinly sliced light Swiss cheese

Place a small nonstick skillet over medium-high heat. Lightly mist with the olive oil spray. Add the mushrooms and garlic and cook, stirring occasionally, for 3 to 5 minutes, or until the mushrooms are tender and any excess moisture is evaporated. Season with salt and pepper. Remove from the heat and cover to keep warm.

In a small bowl, whisk the egg whites with a fork until they bubble lightly.

Place a small nonstick skillet over medium heat. Lightly mist the pan with the olive oil spray. Add the egg whites and cook, lifting the edges with a spatula as they start to set and tipping the pan to allow the uncooked whites to run underneath, for 4 to 6 minutes, or until almost set. Flip the omelet. Arrange the mushrooms and cheese evenly over half of the omelet. Flip the bare half over the filled half and continue cooking until the cheese melts, 1 to 2 minutes. Transfer to a serving plate. Season with additional salt and pepper, if desired, and serve.

Makes 1 serving

Per serving: **131 calories, 23 g protein, 3 g carbohydrates, 3 g fat (2 g saturated), 8 mg cholesterol, trace fiber, 323 mg sodium**

NORTH SEA OMELET

Imitation crabmeat (surimi) is a great way to add lean seafood to your diet without breaking the bank. This omelet is not only tasty, it's colorful and packs plenty of protein, which is definitely needed to help build muscle.

4 large egg whites

¼ teaspoon dried dill

Olive oil spray

¾ ounce (½ cup) finely shredded Cabot's 75% Light Cheddar Cheese

2 ounces (about ½ cup) imitation crabmeat, chopped

1 teaspoon drained capers

2 tablespoons finely chopped scallion

Salt, to taste

Ground black pepper, to taste

In a medium bowl with a fork or small whisk, whisk the egg whites and dill until the egg whites bubble lightly.

Place a small nonstick skillet over medium heat. Lightly mist the pan with the olive oil spray. Add the egg white mixture and cook, lifting the edges with a spatula as they start to set and tipping the pan for the uncooked whites to run underneath, for 4 to 6 minutes, or until almost set. Flip the omelet. Sprinkle the cheese evenly over half of the omelet. Sprinkle the crab, capers, and scallion over the cheese. Flip the bare half over the filled half and continue cooking until the cheese is just melted, 1 to 2 minutes. Transfer to a serving plate. Season with salt and pepper and serve.

Makes 1 serving

Per serving: 184 calories, 29 g protein, 10 g carbohydrates, 3 g fat (1 g saturated), 35 mg cholesterol, less than 1 g fiber, 771 mg sodium

Brady Vilcan, Season 6

I don't know what I would do without low-calorie cooking sprays! They're inexpensive and a great substitute for butter and oils in food preparation. I especially like using sprays to make eggs over easy.

VERY LEMON OATMEAL

If you're a fan of really tart lemony flavor, you'll love this oatmeal. It's light and refreshing, especially in the summer months. If at all possible, it's best to use freshly squeezed lemon juice.

1 cup water

Pinch of salt

½ cup old-fashioned oats

1 tablespoon lemon juice

1 teaspoon dried lemon peel

1 teaspoon honey

½ teaspoon vanilla extract

1 (.035-ounce) packet sugar substitute (such as Splenda)

In a small saucepan, combine the water and salt and bring to a rapid boil over high heat. Add the oats and reduce the heat to medium. Cook, stirring occasionally, for 5 to 7 minutes, or until all the liquid is almost absorbed. Cover, remove from the heat, and let sit for 5 minutes. Stir in the juice, peel, honey, vanilla, and sugar substitute. Transfer to a serving bowl and serve.

Makes 1 serving

Per serving: **196 calories, 7 g protein, 36 g carbohydrates, 3 g fat (0 g saturated), 0 mg cholesterol, 4 g fiber, 75 mg sodium**

Michelle Aguilar, Season 6

I used a lot of lemons while on the ranch. It's a great way to flavor meals and to get in some vitamin C.

SUBTLY STRAWBERRY OATMEAL

I always try to make sure I don't fall into a food rut—it's easy to adopt a healthy way of eating for the long haul if you're constantly changing it up. This simple oatmeal is given a touch of sweetness and a hint of strawberry using 100% fruit spread. Feel free to experiment with other flavors to add even more variety.

1 cup water

Pinch of salt

½ cup old-fashioned oats

½ teaspoon vanilla extract

1½ tablespoons 100% fruit strawberry preserves

In a small saucepan, combine the water and salt and bring to a rapid boil over high heat. Add the oats and reduce the heat to medium. Cook, stirring occasionally, for 5 to 7 minutes, or until all the liquid is almost absorbed. Stir in the vanilla extract. Cover, remove from the heat, and let sit for 5 minutes. Spoon into a serving bowl, stir in the preserves, and serve.

Makes 1 serving

Per serving: 226 calories, 7 g protein, 42 g carbohydrates, 3 g fat (0 g saturated), 0 mg cholesterol, 4 g fiber, 78 mg sodium

Roger Shultz, Season 5 Finalist

When it comes to fueling your body, oatmeal is great as a gasoline for getting you through your workout.

STRAWBERRY-PEACH PARADISE SMOOTHIE

You'll notice here that I don't add much, if any, ice to smoothies. It's best to use frozen fruit to eliminate the need for ice cubes. That way, the finished product will be rich and fruity, not overly watery. (You can buy fresh fruit in season and freeze it yourself or use the packaged varieties.) I mentioned this on my show, Healthy Decadence, *and a number of viewers wrote to me and said that tip solved their smoothie woes, so I thought it might be worth repeating here. In the case of this smoothie, please use freshly squeezed lime juice. It really makes a difference.*

1 cup frozen peach slices

½ cup frozen strawberries

⅔ cup fat-free milk

¼ cup fat-free, sugar-free vanilla yogurt

1 tablespoon freshly squeezed lime juice

In a blender with ice-crushing ability, combine the peach, strawberries, milk, yogurt, and lime juice. Make sure the lid is on tight. Using the Puree or Ice Crush setting, blend until the ingredients are relatively smooth. Then blend on the Liquefy setting or high speed a few seconds until completely smooth. Serve immediately.

Makes 1 serving

Per serving: 181 calories, 9 g protein, 37 g carbohydrates, trace fat (trace saturated), 5 mg cholesterol, 3 g fiber, 126 mg sodium

Biggest Loser Online Club: Jessica Bishop, Season 6

I buy things I can freeze in bulk, such as berries, especially when they're in season. Veggies, too!

Change your life today! Log on to www.biggestloserclub.com and get started

CHERRY-PINEAPPLE SMOOTHIE

A lot of folks go to smoothie bars and think they're doing themselves a favor. My friends and I always used to stop after our long bike rides to enjoy a cold one. But if you've ever glanced at the nutritional info, you know that those smoothies often pack upwards of 600 to 800 calories and tons of sugar—yikes! Here's a toned down smoothie that's just as tasty.

½ cup frozen unsweetened "sweet" cherries

½ cup frozen pineapple chunks

½ cup frozen mango cubes

½ cup fat-free milk

¼ cup fat-free, sugar-free vanilla yogurt

1 teaspoon honey (optional)

In a blender with ice-crushing ability, combine the cherries, pineapple, mango, milk, and yogurt and blend on high speed or the Ice Crush setting until smooth. Stir in the honey, if using, and serve.

Makes 1 serving

Per serving: 232 calories, 9 g protein, 51 g carbohydrates, less than 1 g fat (trace saturated), 4 mg cholesterol, 5 g fiber, 114 mg sodium

APPLE TURNOVER BREAKFAST SUNDAE

The contestants and I are always seeking on-the-go options for breakfast. This is a great one if you pack it in a small resealable plastic container to throw in your cooler bag along with a spoon—it's an easy treat to enjoy after your morning workout or to send to school with the kids.

½ cup fat-free, sugar-free apple turnover–flavored or other apple-flavored yogurt

2 tablespoons crunchy, high-fiber, low-sugar cereal (such as Grape-Nuts)

⅓ cup chopped apple (about ½ small apple)

Pinch of ground cinnamon

1½ teaspoons raisins (optional)

Spoon the yogurt into a small, deep bowl. Sprinkle the cereal over the yogurt, followed by the apple. Top with the cinnamon and then the raisins, if using, and serve.

Makes 1 serving

Per serving: 147 calories, 6 g protein, 31 g carbohydrates, trace fat (trace saturated), 3 mg cholesterol, 3 g fiber, 154 mg sodium

Biggest Loser Online Club: Robyn Klawuhn, Season 6

My teenage son used to eat a muffin or a toaster pastry for breakfast. But since I started *The Biggest Loser* diet, I don't buy those foods. Now he has a peanut butter sandwich and milk or some fruit and yogurt, both of which are less expensive than most processed foods! He actually admits that this type of breakfast makes him feel better in the morning and he's not starving by the time lunch comes around.

Change your life today! Log on to www.biggestloserclub.com and get started

STRAWBERRY BREAKFAST BANANA SPLIT

Though I've maintained a 55-pound weight loss for over 16 years, I proudly eat chocolate every day. Granted, I don't eat a ton of it at any given sitting, but I do incorporate my favorite indulgence into my diet often. This banana split starts my day just how I like it: healthy, happy, and craving-free!

1½ teaspoons fat-free, sugar-free hot fudge

1 small (6") banana, peeled and halved lengthwise

¼ cup fat-free, sugar-free vanilla yogurt

⅓ cup chopped fresh strawberries

1 tablespoon crunchy high-fiber, low-sugar cereal (such as Grape-Nuts)

Heat the hot fudge in the microwave or in the top of a double boiler over simmering water until melted.

Arrange the banana halves in a small banana split dish or shallow bowl with the cut sides facing inward. Spoon the yogurt in the middle. Top with the strawberries, then the cereal. Drizzle the fudge evenly over the top and serve.

Makes 1 serving

Per serving: 195 calories, 5 g protein, 46 g carbohydrates, less than 1 g fat (trace saturated), 2 mg cholesterol, 5 g fiber, 88 mg sodium

4

Lunch: Never Skip It

While some of us may struggle with skipping breakfast, most of us—and especially the Biggest Losers—look forward to lunch. By midday, we're usually hungry and in need of a little downtime. Whether you have a seat at the kitchen table for a few minutes to enjoy a sandwich, gather in a break room with colleagues to gossip over salads, or—in the case of your kids—grab a spot at the cafeteria lunch table, try to use lunch as an opportunity to slow down and savor your food.

It's easy to eat fast food in the car, buy lunch from a vending machine, or grab a handful of something from the fridge, but you'll probably make better food choices—and enjoy your meal more—if you do a little prep work ahead of time and use lunch as an opportunity to recharge for the second half of your day. As trainer Jillian Michaels points out, fueling your body with healthy food in the middle of the day will keep your metabolism on even keel. And you'll probably make better food choices at the end of the day, a danger zone for the lunch-deprived.

Hopefully on weekends, lunch can be a more leisurely affair shared with family and friends, so we've included recipes for heartier dishes as well as grab-and-go meals. And don't forget, leftovers from the previous night's dinner can make a satisfying, economical lunch, too!

When it comes to kids, packing their lunches at home ensures a much healthier meal than the fare they'll find in the cafeteria. For one thing, last time we looked, the vending machines that line the walls of many school cafeterias weren't stocking carrot sticks and fresh fruit. There are efforts under way to improve the nutrition of cafeteria lunches, but many still come in way too high in the fat, sugar, and sodium departments. And, even with healthy choices in the cafeteria line, there may still be the siren call of doughnuts, pizza, cheeseburgers, and, in one case we heard of, French toast on a stick. Packing a lunch for your kids circumvents those temptations. And if you avoid using prepackaged items and prepare these meals yourself, you'll save a lot of bucks over the course of a school year.

To make sure they eat what you send with them, why not let your kids help decide what they'd like for a healthy lunch? Take this book and sit with them for a few minutes. What appeals to them? Inviting your kids to be involved in their own food choices teaches them about good nutrition and makes the experience more fun for them. And don't forget, parents can brown bag it, too. Packing a lunch to take to work will save you money and calories.

The Biggest Loser approach to eating lunch— or really any meal—includes a combination of lean protein, complex carbs, and healthy fat, says Cheryl Forberg, RD, the show's nutritionist. "That could be a big salad with loads of colorful fresh veggies and shredded turkey or chicken, black beans or lentils, shredded reduced-fat cheese, and a flavorful low-fat dressing with a sprinkle of toasted nuts. Or a sandwich made with whole grain bread or a low-fat wrap, also with lots of veggies."

You can even add a piece of fruit or glass of skim or low-fat milk, depending on your calorie budget and whether you're working out before or after lunch. "It sounds like a lot of food," Forberg adds, "but those veggies are high in water and fiber, so they're filling and packed with vitamins and antioxidants."

Depriving yourself of the opportunity to sit down and eat nutritious, satisfying foods in the middle of the day is going to leave you feeling sluggish and out of sorts—and in a frenzied search for French toast on a stick. You've got a lot to accomplish in your afternoon. Feed yourself wisely.

Hearty Weekend Lunches

SALMON BURGERS

These burgers are pretty mild—just the way they should be since they're paired with horseradish mayo. If you plan on eating the burger without the bun and sauce, you'll likely want a stronger flavor. Simply add more horseradish to the salmon mixture before forming the patties.

1 pound boneless, skinless salmon fillets

¼ cup minced sweet onion

¼ cup finely chopped fresh parsley

4 teaspoons prepared horseradish

½ teaspoon Old Bay 30% Less Sodium Seasoning

4 tablespoons low-fat mayonnaise

4 whole grain or whole wheat hamburger buns, split, toasted if desired

4 small green-leaf lettuce leaves

4 large or 8 small thin slices tomato

Cut the salmon into cubes and place in a food processor fitted with a chopping blade. Pulse until the salmon is about the consistency of ground beef. Transfer to a medium mixing bowl and stir in the onion, parsley, 2 teaspoons of the horseradish, and the Old Bay.

Divide the mixture into 4 equal portions and shape into patties that are about 4" in diameter.

Place a large nonstick skillet over medium-high heat. When hot, add the patties and cook for 2 to 3 minutes per side, or until the outsides are lightly browned and the patties are cooked through (they should be pale pink throughout).

Meanwhile, mix the mayonnaise with the remaining 2 teaspoons horseradish until well combined. Set aside.

Place each bun bottom on a plate. Top with the patties followed by the lettuce and tomato. Spread one-fourth of the mayo mixture (about 1 tablespoon each) on each bun top, flip atop the patties, and serve.

Makes 4 servings

Per serving: 362 calories, 27 g protein, 27 g carbohydrates, 16 g fat (3 g saturated), 67 mg cholesterol, 4 g fiber, 346 mg sodium

BLT BURGERS

Though you might be tempted to try to save money by buying 93% lean ground beef instead of 96% lean, don't. Though they don't sound very different, 93% lean has almost twice the fat of 96%. One 4-ounce serving of 93% lean has about 180 calories and 8 grams of fat. The 96% lean has 150 calories and only 4½ grams of fat.

4 strips extra-lean turkey bacon, each cut in half

1 pound 96% lean ground beef

4 whole grain or whole wheat hamburger buns, split

1 cup chopped fresh spinach leaves

4 large or 8 to 12 small thin tomato slices

4 tablespoons low-fat mayonnaise

Preheat a grill to high heat.

Place a medium nonstick skillet over medium-high heat and add the bacon strips. Cook for 2 to 3 minutes per side, or until crisp. Remove from the pan and cover to keep warm.

Divide the beef into 4 equal portions and shape into balls, packing them tightly as you do. Press each into a patty that is about ½" larger than the diameter of the buns.

Grill the burgers for about 2 minutes per side for medium rare, or until desired doneness (do not smash the burgers with a spatula). Place the bun halves, cut sides down, on the upper grill rack or away from direct flame until toasted, about 20 seconds.

Place each toasted bun bottom on a plate. Top with the spinach, tomato, patties, then 2 pieces of bacon each. Spread 1 tablespoon mayonnaise evenly on each bun top, flip atop the patties, and serve.

Makes 4 servings

Per serving: 295 calories, 29 g protein, 25 g carbohydrates, 9 g fat (2 g saturated), 70 mg cholesterol, 4 g fiber, 547 mg sodium

PIZZA BURGERS

A lot of people think that low-fat cheese doesn't taste good. In many cases, they're absolutely right. But, thank goodness, that's not true of all brands. Some are so good I find them addictive, while others I wouldn't eat if you paid me. Find a brand you like and stick with it. And remember that if you don't like it before you combine it with other ingredients, you're certainly not going to like it afterwards.

1 pound 96% lean ground beef

1 teaspoon dried oregano

½ teaspoon garlic powder

½ to 1 teaspoon crushed red pepper flakes, or to taste

¼ teaspoon salt

3 ounces low-fat mozzarella cheese, thinly sliced

½ cup Main Event Marinara Sauce (page 162) or other low-fat, lower-sodium, low-sugar marinara sauce

4 whole grain or whole wheat hamburger buns, split

Preheat a grill to high heat.

In a large bowl, mix the beef, oregano, garlic powder, red pepper flakes, and salt until well combined. Divide the mixture into 4 equal portions and shape into balls, packing them tightly as you do. Press each into a patty that is about ½" larger than the diameter of the buns.

Grill the burgers for about 2 minutes per side for medium rare, or until desired doneness (do not smash the burgers with a spatula). About 1 minute before they are done, divide the cheese slices among the tops and let melt.

Meanwhile, spoon the sauce into a medium microwave-safe bowl. Microwave on low until hot, 30 to 60 seconds. Place the bun halves, cut sides down, on an upper grill rack or away from direct flame for about 20 seconds, or until toasted.

Place each bun bottom on a serving plate, toasted side up. Place the patties, cheese side up, on top of the bun bottoms. Spread 2 tablespoons sauce on each bun top, flip atop the patties, and serve.

Makes 4 servings

Per serving: 304 calories, 32 g protein, 27 g carbohydrates, 9 g fat (3 g saturated), 68 mg cholesterol, 5 g fiber, 605 mg sodium

FRENCH ONION BAGEL BURGERS

For a change, I like to use high-fiber, low-fat bagels for burgers—they're a great healthy alternative to hamburger buns. Weight Watchers and Western Bagel make a number of high-fiber varieties (I love the onion ones!). However, if they're too pricey or you can't find them, you can use whole wheat or whole grain hamburger buns . . . just keep in mind that you'll be cutting out about 6 grams of fiber per burger.

---

1 pound 96% lean ground beef

Salt, to taste

Ground black pepper, to taste

4 high-fiber, low-fat bagels (I used Weight Watchers brand), split

4 small green-leaf lettuce leaves

12 thin slices plum tomatoes

4 (¾-ounce) Laughing Cow Light French Onion cheese wedges

Preheat a grill to high heat.

Divide the beef into 4 equal portions and shape into balls, packing them tightly as you do. Press each into a patty that is about ½" larger in diameter than the bagels. Season with salt and pepper.

Grill the burgers for 1 to 2 minutes per side for medium rare, or until desired doneness (do not smash the burgers with a spatula). If desired, place the bagel halves, cut sides down, on the upper grill rack or away from direct flame for about 20 seconds, until just toasted.

Place each bagel bottom on a plate. Top with the lettuce and tomatoes, followed by the patties. Spread the inside of each bagel top evenly with 1 cheese wedge, flip the bagel tops atop the burgers, and serve.

Makes 4 servings

Per serving: 329 calories, 34 g protein, 36 g carbohydrates, 7 g fat (3 g saturated), 70 mg cholesterol, 10 g fiber, 695 mg sodium

Paul Marks, Season 5

Coming from someone who has never cooked—it's amazing how much fun cooking can be when you incorporate the entire family!

RANCH BURGER POCKET

I often make pocket sandwiches and open wraps or burritos with tortillas. In order to get a healthful meal with plenty of lean protein and veggies, you'd need a huge tortilla (with too many carbs) to enclose it all. By keeping the delicious tortillas open, you get to have your burger and eat it too . . . consequence-free.

4 ounces 96% lean ground beef

Ground black pepper, to taste (optional)

1 (7½") low-fat, low-carb, multigrain or whole wheat tortilla

1 tablespoon low-fat ranch dressing (I used the Follow Your Heart brand)

¼ cup chopped spinach leaves

3 thin slices Roma tomato

1 very thin slice onion

Preheat a grill to high heat.

Pack the beef tightly together then shape into a rectangle that is about 3½" by 4". Season with pepper, if desired.

Grill the burger for about 45 seconds per side for medium-rare, or until desired doneness (do not smash the burger with a spatula).

Place the tortilla on a serving plate. Picture the tortilla as a clock and place the burger patty so that the center of one of the shorter sides starts at 12:00 and the patty stretches down the center of the tortilla. Top the burger with the dressing, spinach, tomato, and onion slice. Fold the bare end of the tortilla up over the filling, and then fold the sides of the tortilla over the middle. Serve immediately.

Makes 1 serving

Per serving: 257 calories, 30 g protein, 16 g carbohydrates, 8 g fat (2 g saturated), 60 mg cholesterol, 9 g fiber, 268 mg sodium

Neill Harmer, Season 5

Don't let junk food be your crutch anymore. It's amazing how inexpensive it can be to eat healthy food. In fact, the good, nutritious food makes you fuller faster, but without as many calories as the bad stuff.

MEATBALL LOVERS' MUST-HAVE FAMILY-SIZED MEATBALL PARMESAN SUB

This sub is so jam-packed with meatballs, no one will ever guess it came from a healthy cookbook. In fact, it has so many meatballs, it's almost hard to get them all stuffed into the baguette—just the way I love it!

1   (8-ounce) whole wheat or multigrain baguette

New Favorite Meatballs (page 87)

1½ cups Main Event Marinara Sauce (page 162)

1½ tablespoons grated reduced-fat Parmesan cheese

Preheat the oven to 400°F.

Cut a piece of aluminum foil a couple of inches longer than the baguette. Turn the baguette on its side and cut the entire length, not cutting all of the way through, as you would cut a roll to make a sandwich. Wrap the baguette in the foil so it is completely covered. Place the baguette in the oven to warm, about 10 minutes.

Meanwhile, in a medium nonstick saucepan over low heat or in a large microwave-safe bowl or dish in the microwave, reheat the meatballs in the sauce until hot.

Unwrap the baguette. Open it carefully, being sure not to burn yourself or break apart the 2 halves. Spoon the warmed meatballs and sauce into the baguette. Sprinkle the Parmesan evenly over the meatballs. Cut crosswise into 4 equal sandwiches and serve.

Makes 4 servings

Per serving: 395 calories, 34 g protein, 48 g carbohydrates, 8 g fat (2 g saturated), 63 mg cholesterol, 6 g fiber, 644 mg sodium

GRILLED CHICKEN SMOTHERED NACHOS

To save money and calories, skip buying the grilled chicken breast at the store and make Simple Grilled Chicken (page 126) instead: Just follow the recipe exactly, swapping out the garlic and herb seasoning for a Mexican or Southwest seasoning (I use Mrs. Dash Southwest Chipotle).

Also, be sure you either wear gloves or wash your hands immediately after working with jalapeños. Though you're sure to love this dish, you won't enjoy it nearly as much if your jalapeño-affected hands make even minimal contact with your eyes.

---

1 ounce baked tortilla chips (I used Guiltless Gourmet)

¼ cup drained canned 50% less-sodium black beans, heated

4 ounces grilled extra-lean boneless, skinless chicken breast, cut into small cubes, reheated if necessary

2 tablespoons salsa con queso, all natural if possible (I used Salpica), heated

3 tablespoons finely chopped seeded tomato

2 tablespoons thinly sliced jalapeño chile pepper (wear plastic gloves when handling)

Lay the chips on a dinner plate. Top them evenly with the beans, followed by the chicken. Drizzle the salsa con queso evenly over the top. Top with the tomato and jalapeño slices and serve.

Makes 1 serving

Per serving: 321 calories, 32 g protein, 36 g carbohydrates, 5 g fat (less than 1 g saturated), 65 mg cholesterol, 5 g fiber, 498 mg sodium

Budget Tips from The Biggest Loser

Don't let meal scraps go to waste. If your kids aren't going to eat the leftovers on their plates, can Fido? Dog food is expensive! And after all, he's part of the family, too.

BLACK BEAN SOUP

If you don't have an immersion blender, don't worry. You can still make this recipe. Just bring the mixture to a simmer for a minute then transfer to a traditional blender or food processor and puree. Be sure to put the lid on tight and drape a towel over the top of the blender, then hold to keep in place as you blend. Once it's smooth, you can pour it back into the saucepan and continue.

2 (15-ounce) cans 50% less-sodium black beans, drained

1 (14.5-ounce) can diced tomatoes in juice

2 cups water

¾ cup minced celery

¾ cup minced onion

2 teaspoons finely chopped seeded jalapeño chile pepper (wear plastic gloves when handling)

1 teaspoon freshly minced garlic

1 teaspoon ground cumin

Ground black pepper, to taste

Red pepper flakes, to taste

In a large nonstick saucepan, combine three-fourths of the black beans, one-half of the tomatoes, and the water and bring to a simmer over medium heat. With an immersion blender, puree until mostly smooth. (*Note:* When using an immersion blender, make sure not to scratch the bottom of your nonstick pan.)

Add the remaining black beans and tomatoes, along with the celery, onion, jalapeño, garlic, and cumin. Season with black pepper and red pepper flakes. Cover the pot, leaving the lid slightly ajar for steam to escape, and reduce the heat to low. Simmer for 20 to 25 minutes longer, or until the vegetables are tender. Divide the soup evenly among 6 soup bowls and serve.

Makes 6 (1-cup) servings

Per serving: 102 calories, 7 g protein, 24 g carbohydrates, trace fat (trace saturated), 0 mg cholesterol, 7 g fiber, 489 mg sodium

Biggest Loser Online Club: Kathy Robb, Season 6

Try eating soups, stews, and salads as a main course. This way you are getting quantity as well as higher-fiber items. And you can freeze soups and stews once they cool—they will last for about 3 months in the freezer.

CURRIED SPLIT-PEA SOUP

This is a very hearty, rich, and thick soup that is perfect for the cold winter months. If you'd prefer your soup a bit thinner, just add a little more milk.

1 cup dried split peas, rinsed

4 cups water

1 tablespoon extra-virgin olive oil

2 medium stalks celery, diced

½ cup diced sweet onion

½ extra-large (5-gram) vegetable bouillon cube

1½ teaspoons curry powder

1 medium carrot, peeled and diced

¼ cup fat-free milk

Ground black pepper, to taste

In a medium nonstick saucepan, combine the peas and water and bring to a boil over medium-high heat. Reduce the heat and simmer until the peas are soft, about 30 minutes, or according to package directions.

Meanwhile, heat the oil in a medium nonstick skillet over medium-high heat. When hot, add the celery and onion and cook, stirring occasionally, until the onion is translucent and the celery is tender but not browned, 5 to 7 minutes.

When the peas are tender, add the celery mixture to the saucepan, along with the bouillon and curry powder. With an immersion blender, puree the soup just until smooth. (Note: When using an immersion blender, make sure not to scratch the bottom of your nonstick pan.)

Add the carrot to the soup and slowly bring to a boil. Simmer just until the carrot is tender, 6 to 8 minutes. Remove the pan from the heat and slowly stir in the milk. Season with pepper. Divide the soup among 4 soup bowls and serve.

Makes 4 (³⁄₄-cup) servings

Per serving: 230 calories, 13 g protein, 36 g carbohydrates, 5 g fat (less than 1 g saturated), trace cholesterol, 14 g fiber, 264 mg sodium

FAMILY-SIZED ROAST BEEF SUB

This sandwich tastes great using any lean deli roast beef, leftover lean pot roast, or London broil. I often make it as written here or use leftover Gym Rat's Grilled London Broil (page 148). Either option saves tons of sodium—and tons of cash—compared to roast beef bought at the deli counter. This recipe yields four sandwiches so it's an easy way to make packable lunches for the whole family.

---

1 (8-ounce) whole wheat or multigrain baguette

¼ cup low-fat mayonnaise

Dried oregano, to taste

1 large tomato, thinly sliced

¾ cup loosely packed spinach leaves, stems removed

¾ cup green bell pepper strips

½ cup onion slivers

2 tablespoons sliced black olives

1 pound very thinly sliced Peppered Pot Roast (page 145) or other extra-lean roast beef

Salt, to taste

Ground black pepper, to taste

Red pepper flakes, to taste

Turn the baguette on its side and cut the entire length, not cutting all of the way through, as you would cut a roll to make a sandwich. Open it carefully, being sure not to break apart the 2 halves. Spread the mayo evenly over the inside. Sprinkle the oregano over the mayonnaise. Add the tomato, spinach, bell pepper, onion, olives, and then the beef, packing it into the sandwich. Season with the salt, black pepper, and red pepper flakes. Close the sandwich, cut it crosswise into 4 equal sandwiches, and serve.

Makes 4 servings

Per serving: 309 calories, 30 g protein, 34 g carbohydrates, 8 g fat (2 g saturated), 49 mg cholesterol, 4 fiber, 384 mg sodium

PORK SANDWICH

I've always loved coleslaw on pork sandwiches. Although I particularly love this sandwich with the coleslaw recipe from this book (see page 181), any lean coleslaw will work.

2 slices sesame sprouted grain bread or whole grain bread (I used the Ezekiel 4:9 brand)

4 ounces thinly sliced Herbed Pork Loin Roast (page 159)

⅓ cup Coleslaw with Orange-Cilantro Vinaigrette (page 181), slightly drained

Lay one bread slice on a serving plate. Top with the pork, followed by the coleslaw. Place the remaining bread slice atop the sandwich and serve.

Makes 1 serving

Per serving: 318 calories, 32 g protein, 32 g carbohydrates, 5 g fat (1 g saturated), 74 mg cholesterol, 7 g fiber, 316 mg sodium

Budget Tips from The Biggest Loser

Fresh, whole-grain bread from the bakery can go stale quickly. But day-old breads can be a good bargain. Try buying a loaf at a reduced price. Slice it immediately and toast for sandwiches or pop it in the freezer for later use.

BBQ-BACON MEAT LOAF SANDWICH

What is it about the combo of bacon and barbecue sauce that just piques everyone's appetites? It's clearly a winning combo, so I was determined to pair them once again, this time in a sandwich.

2 slices sesame sprouted grain bread or whole grain bread (I used the Ezekiel 4:9 brand)

1½ slices BBQ-Bacon Meat Loaf (page 124)

¼ cup spinach leaves, stems removed

3 (¼"-thick) slices plum tomato

2 very thin slices red onion

1 tablespoon low-fat mayonnaise

Lay one bread slice on a serving plate. Top it evenly with the meat loaf, followed by the spinach, then the tomato and onion. Spread the mayonnaise evenly over the remaining bread slice, flip it atop the sandwich, and serve.

Makes 1 serving

Per serving: 399 calories, 35 g protein, 50 g carbohydrates, 5 g fat (less than 1 g saturated), 57 mg cholesterol, 9 g fiber, 699 mg sodium

Adam and Stacey Capers, Season 6

We pack sandwiches on whole wheat bread, with lean meats and low-fat cheese. Our daughter loves fruits and vegetables, so we pack her favorites—carrots, celery, strawberries, cherries—for her to have as snacks. As a special treat, we pack baked versions of her favorites goodies, like potato chips and crackers.

TURKEY AND SWISS SANDWICH WITH SWEET MUSTARD

I sometimes feel silly including recipes for common items like a turkey and Swiss sandwich in my cookbooks. But I also realize how important it is for people to know, with ease, how many calories are really in their favorite sandwiches. Although I'm generally not a fan of sprouted grain bread, I do really enjoy Ezekiel's sesame sprouted grain when I get it fresh. So we used that to calculate the nutritional information for this sandwich. You can use whole grain or whole wheat, but you won't be getting as much fiber.

2 slices sesame sprouted grain or whole grain bread (I used the Ezekiel 4:9 brand)

4 ounces Buffalo Turkey-Breast Roast (page 127) or extra-lean, low-sodium deli turkey, thinly sliced

½ ounce light Swiss cheese slivers or slices (I used Sargento)

¼ cup fresh spinach leaves, stems removed

3 (¼"-thick) slices plum tomato

2 very thin slices red onion

2 teaspoons honey mustard, or more to taste

Lay one bread slice on a serving plate. Top it with the turkey, followed by the cheese, then the spinach, tomato, and onion. Spread the mustard evenly over the remaining bread slice, flip it atop the sandwich, and serve.

Makes 1 serving

Per serving: 367 calories, 41 g protein, 38 g carbohydrates, 6 g fat (1 g saturated), 49 mg cholesterol, 8 g fiber, 484 mg sodium

MEDITERRANEAN CHICKEN SANDWICH

I'm a huge fan of substituting yogurt for mayo—granted, I only do that when meticulously combining flavors or it's bound to fail. But in this recipe, it's a great way to add moisture to the sandwich, stretching the amount of hummus without adding too much fat.

---

1 tablespoon prepared roasted red pepper (or any flavor) hummus

1½ teaspoons fat-free plain yogurt

2 slices sesame sprouted grain bread or whole grain bread (I used the Ezekiel 4:9 brand)

4 ounces Simple Grilled Chicken (page 126), thinly sliced

⅓ cup loosely packed fresh spinach leaves, stems removed

3 (¼"-thick) slices plum tomato

4 slices cucumber

2 very thin slices red onion

In a small bowl, stir together the hummus and yogurt until well combined.

Lay one bread slice on a serving plate. Top it evenly with the chicken, then the spinach, cucumber, tomato, and onion. Spread the hummus mixture evenly over the remaining bread slice and flip it atop the sandwich. Serve immediately, or wrap in plastic wrap and refrigerate for up to 1 day.

Makes 1 serving

Per serving: 340 calories, 36 g protein, 39 g carbohydrates, 4 g fat (trace saturated), 65 mg cholesterol, 8 g fiber, 324 mg sodium

CHICKEN SALAD DIJON WITH GRAPES AND APPLE

Dijon mustard lovers will love this twist on traditional chicken salad—and will also be shocked by the creaminess of the dressing, given that it has about one-third of the calories and one-fourth of the fat usually found in a similar sized serving. Serve over a bed of butter lettuce or fresh spinach, or on sprouted grain or multigrain bread.

1 **pound trimmed boneless, skinless chicken breasts**

3 **teaspoons extra-virgin olive oil**

Salt, to taste

Ground black pepper, to taste

3 **tablespoons fat-free plain yogurt**

3 **tablespoons Dijon mustard**

⅓ **cup chopped celery**

⅓ **cup seedless grapes, each cut in half**

⅓ **cup chopped red apple**

Preheat a grill to high heat.

Rub the chicken all over with 1 teaspoon of the olive oil and season with salt and pepper. Place on the grill and cook for 3 to 5 minutes per side, or until the chicken is no longer pink and juices run clear. Allow the chicken to cool, then cut it into bite-sized cubes.

In a large glass or plastic mixing bowl, whisk together the remaining 2 teaspoons olive oil, the yogurt, and mustard. Add the chicken, celery, grapes, and apple. Gently toss well to combine. Season with salt and pepper and serve.

Makes 4 servings

Per serving: 173 calories, 27 g protein, 4 g carbohydrates, 5 g fat (less than 1 g saturated), 66 mg cholesterol, trace fiber, 361 mg sodium

Budget Tips from The Biggest Loser

Look for large family packs of chicken breasts, especially when they are on sale. You can divide the chicken into single or family-sized portions in freezer bags and defrost as necessary.

OLD BAY SHRIMP LETTUCE WRAPS

I use bay shrimp here to save money. But if larger, cooked shrimp are on sale (or you live in a part of the country where it's inexpensive to buy them raw and steam and chill them yourself), feel free to swap those in, as shown here. This really simple salad is extra-light and fun since you serve it in lettuce cups.

2 tablespoons low-fat mayonnaise

2 tablespoons fat-free plain yogurt

2 teaspoons freshly squeezed lemon juice

1 teaspoon Old Bay 30% Less Sodium Seasoning

1 pound cooked peeled bay shrimp, thoroughly drained

12 Bibb lettuce leaves

In a large bowl, mix the mayonnaise, yogurt, lemon juice, and Old Bay until well combined. Add the shrimp and mix thoroughly.

Place all 12 lettuce leaves on a large platter or place 3 leaves on each of 4 serving plates. Evenly divide the shrimp mixture (about 3 tablespoons each) among the centers of the lettuce leaves. Serve immediately.

Makes 4 (3-wrap) servings

Per serving: 182 calories, 14 g protein, 3 g carbohydrates, 1 g fat (trace saturated), 127 mg cholesterol, less than 1 g fiber, 314 mg sodium

From the Experts

Yes, it takes more time, but when you prepare a dish at home rather than picking up a premade version, you can save on costs by 50 percent or more. It also ensures that your dish is healthier because you dictate the amount of oil and salt it contains. And, best of all, this guarantees that the food contains no hidden preservatives.

—Cheryl Forberg, RD, nutritionist for *The Biggest Loser*

TODAY'S TUNA SANDWICHES

People often order tuna sandwiches thinking that they're healthy. Well . . . the tuna is, but until you've made tuna salad yourself a number of times, you have no idea how much mayo can be packed into a small serving. Heck, you could literally eat a can of tuna, then a few pieces of fudge, and barely consume as much fat as you would eating a tuna sandwich from your typical sub shop.

---

2 (6-ounce) cans chunk light tuna in water, drained

3 tablespoons low-fat mayonnaise

¼ cup finely chopped celery

¼ cup finely chopped red onion

Ground black pepper, to taste

8 slices sesame sprouted grain bread or whole grain bread (I used the Ezekiel 4:9 brand)

16 thin slices tomato

16 thin slices cucumber

1⅓ cups alfalfa sprouts

In a medium bowl, mix the tuna with the mayonnaise until well combined. Stir in the celery and onion and season with pepper.

Place one piece of bread on each of 4 serving plates. Evenly place 4 slices of tomato, followed by 4 slices of cucumber on each bread slice. Top each with one-fourth of the tuna mixture (about ¼ cup + 2 tablespoons each), followed by one-fourth of the alfalfa sprouts. Top each sandwich with a remaining bread slice and serve.

Makes 4 servings

Per serving: 284 calories, 27 g protein, 34 g carbohydrates, 3 g fat (trace saturated), 21 mg cholesterol, 7 g fiber, 410 mg sodium

Brittany Aberle, Season 5

Be sure to drink water all day long. It's much better for you than diet soda, and unlike juice, it has zero calories.

SALMON SPINACH SALAD

I've used spinach in most of the salads in this book because Dr. Dansinger encourages the contestants to eat as much fiber as possible. And he encourages me to help them (and you!) with these recipes. I actually love raw spinach—plus, it's often much more affordable than mixed baby greens or even Romaine lettuce, neither of which have as many nutrients. If it's on sale and you like bolder flavors, arugula is another delicious option for this salad. Though it definitely has a more bitter taste, it's one of the few bitter greens I actually love. If you've never had it, next time you're at your grocery store, ask the produce guy or gal to give you a leaf. You may be surprised how much you enjoy it. If you don't, you haven't wasted any hard-earned cash.

16 cups loosely packed spinach leaves, stems removed

¾ cup red onion slivers

6 tablespoons light honey mustard dressing

¾ recipe Basic Pan-Seared Salmon (page 143)

In a large salad bowl, toss the spinach and onion with the dressing. Divide the mixture among 4 serving plates. Top each salad with one-fourth of the salmon (about 3 ounces) and serve immediately.

Makes 4 servings

Per serving: 253 calories, 20 g protein, 19 g carbohydrates, 12 g fat (2 g saturated), 50 mg cholesterol, 5 g fiber, 408 mg sodium

Michelle Aguilar, Season 6

One thing I have learned is that you *have* to get organized—knowing what you have in your kitchen is vital to living on a budget. When you are headed out to the store, you have to make a list. It's a must!

BERRY MIXED GREEN SALAD WITH GRILLED CHICKEN

A lunch spot in L.A. that I love to visit (in the rare instances that I'm not cooking) serves the best green salads. They add all sorts of fresh fruits and herbs to what would otherwise be pretty plain offerings. This salad is inspired by one of my faves there. Feel free to use raspberries instead of the strawberries if they're in season and on sale. They're equally delicious.

12 cups mixed baby greens

1½ cups cored, sliced strawberries

1½ ounces very finely crumbled goat cheese

6 tablespoons light raspberry vinaigrette

Simple Grilled Chicken (page 126) or 1 pound other lean grilled chicken breast, sliced

In a large bowl, combine the greens, strawberries, and cheese. Pour the vinaigrette over the mixture and toss. Divide the salad among 4 dinner plates or large salad bowls. Top each with one-fourth of the chicken (about 4 ounces) and serve.

Makes 4 servings

Per serving: 242 calories, 30 g protein, 13 g carbohydrates, 8 g fat (2 g saturated), 71 mg cholesterol, 3 g fiber, 225 mg sodium

Biggest Loser Trainer Tip: Bob Harper

It's so important to get the nutrient-dense green veggies featured in these recipes. They're a great source of fiber and carbohydrates, and they're going to fill you up!

SPINACH SALAD WITH FETA AND MANDARIN ORANGES

I'm generally not a fan of Mandarin oranges in salads (I worry they'll make the salad soggy), but somehow this combo has recently become one of my favorites. The sweetness of the oranges and the saltiness of the feta coupled with lean protein and fresh spinach keep my cravings satisfied—and will do the same for you! Just be sure, here, as always, to dry your raw veggies well. It's the only way you'll achieve restaurant-quality salads.

---

14 cups loosely packed spinach leaves, stems removed

1 (10½-ounce) can unsweetened mandarin oranges in juice, drained (about 1 cup)

1½ ounces finely crumbled reduced-fat feta cheese

½ cup red onion slivers

6 tablespoons light balsamic vinaigrette

Simple Grilled Chicken (page 126) or 1 pound other lean grilled chicken breast, cut into strips

In a large salad bowl, combine the spinach, oranges, feta, and onion. Pour the vinaigrette over the mixture and toss. Divide the salad among 4 dinner plates or large salad bowls. Top each with one-fourth of the chicken (about 4 ounces) and serve.

Makes 4 servings

Per serving: 240 calories, 31 g protein, 17 g carbohydrates, 6 g fat (2 g saturated), 68 mg cholesterol, 5 g fiber, 469 g sodium

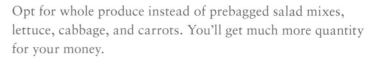

Budget Tips from The Biggest Loser

Opt for whole produce instead of prebagged salad mixes, lettuce, cabbage, and carrots. You'll get much more quantity for your money.

GREEK SALAD WITH GRILLED CHICKEN

Over the past couple of years, I've ordered Greek salad at a number of Greek restaurants and many of them have been accompanied by a vinaigrette with a strong yellow mustard taste. I started craving that dressing and decided to remake it since I know that dressings from restaurants can be really fattening. Below is the result. If you haven't had a lot of fat in your day, you can throw in a few Greek olives to make the salad even more heavenly. But either way, if you love yellow mustard, you'll love this salad.

12 cups chopped fresh
spinach leaves

3 cups chopped tomatoes

2 cups chopped cucumber

3 ounces crumbled reduced-
fat feta cheese

Greek Vinaigrette
(opposite page)

Simple Grilled Chicken
(page 126) or 1 pound
other lean grilled chicken
breast, sliced

In a large glass or plastic bowl, combine the spinach, tomatoes, cucumber, and feta. Pour the vinaigrette over the mixture and toss. Divide the salad among 4 dinner plates or large salad bowls. Top each with one-fourth of the chicken (about 4 ounces) and serve.

Makes 4 servings

Per serving: 268 calories, 35 g protein, 14 g carbohydrates, 9 g fat
(3 g saturated), 72 mg cholesterol, 4 g fiber, 637 mg sodium

Biggest Loser Online Club: Anne Kidney, Season 6

Each week I pick the local grocery store with the most items on sale that we need and then cross-reference the coupons I have. I even get my mom's hand-me-down coupons each week, after she's cut out whatever she needs. It's become a game! My lowest savings score was 10 percent; my biggest savings ever was about 42 percent with the free turkey at Thanksgiving last year!

Change your life today! Log on to www.biggestloserclub.com and get started

GREEK VINAIGRETTE

3 tablespoons yellow mustard

2 tablespoons apple cider vinegar

1 tablespoon fat-free plain yogurt

1½ teaspoons honey

1 tablespoon extra-virgin olive oil

2 tablespoons minced onion

1 teaspoon freshly minced garlic

Pinch of salt

Ground black pepper, to taste

In a medium resealable plastic container, whisk together the mustard, vinegar, yogurt, and honey. Slowly whisk in the oil. Stir in the onion and garlic, then season with salt and pepper. Serve immediately or store in the refrigerator for up to 5 days.

Makes 4 (2-tablespoon) servings

Per serving: 44 calories, trace protein, 3 g carbohydrates, 4 g fat (trace saturated), trace cholesterol, trace fiber, 311 mg sodium

5

Snacks: Eat to Lose

You've seen it happen countless times. In the midst of a challenging workout, the contestants begin to wilt before your eyes. Their bodies slump, their eyes cloud over, and they enter the land of slow motion. Then Bob or Jillian jumps in the picture and yells, "Did you eat? Did you eat?!" Translation: Did you fuel up your tank before you walked in here?

When you're trying to lose weight, it's never a good idea to starve yourself. Not getting enough energy is one of the worst possible moves you can make, as the contestants quickly learn. This is where healthy snacking comes in.

The Biggest Loser eating plan is structured around eating three meals and two snacks a day. Depending on your calorie budget, each snack can range from 150 to 180 calories, says Cheryl Forberg, RD, nutritionist for *The Biggest Loser*. Snacks should be eaten during that energy slump time, a few hours after each of your first two scheduled daily meals. The idea is to eat something about every 3 to 4 hours, which will help keep cravings at bay, blood sugar stable, and your energy up. Otherwise, you risk getting overly hungry and being one doughnut away from a slip.

Forberg encourages the contestants to have a snack that combines one serving of carbohydrates (a piece of fruit, for example) with a half serving of protein (such as a low-fat cheese stick). That protein will help you feel full and satisfied, and when combined with the carbs, it will keep blood sugar from plummeting.

Coleen Skeabeck of Season 6 confesses she was a snackaholic: Ice cream and sweets were her usual choices. When she decided to lose weight, she needed to learn healthy ways to snack. "My favorite snacks now are simple and affordable," she says. They include hummus and baby carrots, or an apple or blueberries with a handful of raw almonds. "Occasionally, I'll slice up a cucumber and squeeze a little lemon on it—very refreshing! All these snacks are perfect for giving yourself a little energy and are easy to take on the go."

As you'll read time and time again in this book, plastic bags are your best buddies when it comes to snacks. Use them to preportion your snacks so you can grab and go, tossing your afternoon energy boost into your bag on the way to work or school. It's also smart to keep preportioned snacks in the fridge in plastic bags or reusable containers—they're handy for preworkout pick-me-ups and postgym refueling.

BiggestLoserClub.com member Juliana O'Hare has converted a neighborhood of teens to healthy snacking. She cuts up some of her fresh fruits and vegetables after getting home from the grocery store and puts them in snack-size bags for work. "I noticed that my cleverly packaged healthy snacks kept disappearing from my refrigerator. I asked my boys (who are 12 and 13) about it, and they told me that all their friends now come to our house because they love that there are always fresh fruits and veggies cut up in the fridge. They will take a break from skateboarding or playing basketball and come over and eat. My irritation subsided when I realized that I was introducing my kids and their friends to healthy snacking habits."

So go ahead and dig into some of the easy, satisfying snack recipes that follow and start your own delicious snack habit today!

OPEN-FACED ROAST BEEF SANDWICH

In this book, I use spinach in many recipes for burgers, sandwiches, salads, and more. I choose spinach so often because it's one of the more mild-tasting dark leafy greens—the darker, the more nutrients—and also because it's less expensive than many other dark greens. You can substitute any green that you or your family like in this sandwich if you are tired of spinach . . . but remember, the darker, the better.

1 slice sesame sprouted grain or whole grain bread (I used Ezekiel's 4:9)

1 (¾-ounce) Light Swiss Original Laughing Cow cheese wedge

¼ cup loosely packed spinach leaves, stems removed

4 thin slices plum tomato

3 ounces Gym Rat's Grilled London Broil (page 148) or other extra-lean roast beef, very thinly sliced

2 small green olives with pimientos (sometimes called manzillas), each cut into 3 slices

Place the bread slice on a serving plate and spread evenly with the cheese. Cut in half diagonally and top each half evenly with the spinach, then the tomato and beef. Evenly space the olive slices on top of the beef and serve.

Makes 1 serving

Per serving: 232 calories, 25 g protein, 21 g carbohydrates, 7 g fat (2 g saturated), 47 mg cholesterol, 4 g fiber, 630 mg sodium

Isabeau Miller, Season 4 Finalist

Have healthy snacks nearby when you work out. That way you can take a break, grab something to help you refuel, and you don't have to stop your momentum entirely.

FIESTA TURKEY MINI-TOSTADAS

If you want to save a bit more money and the Tostitos aren't on sale, you can buy any baked tortilla chips to serve with the turkey. You won't have pretty little tostadas, but it's a delicious snack regardless. And if you're looking to save time, simply divide the cooked turkey mixture among 4 bowls and serve with a side of the scoops or chips.

40 Baked Tostitos Scoops

Olive oil spray

1 pound extra-lean ground turkey breast

Salt, to taste

Ground black pepper, to taste

¾ to 1 cup mild, medium, or hot salsa, to taste

Place 10 scoops on each of 4 dinner plates or all 40 scoops on a serving platter.

Place a large nonstick skillet over medium-high heat. When hot, lightly coat with the olive oil spray and add the turkey. Season with salt and pepper. Cook, breaking the turkey into bite-sized chunks and stirring with a spatula or wooden spoon, until no longer pink, 3 to 5 minutes. Stir in the salsa. Divide the mixture evenly among the scoops (about 1 heaping tablespoon each) and serve.

Makes 4 servings

Per serving: 208 calories, 29 g protein, 18 g carbohydrates, 4 g fat (trace saturated), 45 mg cholesterol, 1 g fiber, 188 mg sodium

Budget Tips from The Biggest Loser

Write it down! Keep a small pad in your kitchen so you can note what items you need to buy as soon as you run out. That way you won't have to make multiple trips to the grocery store, which always seem to result in unplanned purchasing.

THIN AND CRISPY GOURMET HULA PIZZA

I don't think I'm capable of writing a book without including at least one pizza. I mean, come on—it's not American to completely give up pizza! By using a low-fat, whole wheat tortilla as the crust (please do not attempt this recipe with a low-carb tortilla), you can enjoy a thin and crispy pizza without guilt. Once you've mastered this pizza, feel free to create your own thin and crispy pizza with Main Event Marinara Sauce (page 162), low-fat cheese, and plenty of lean protein and veggies. Your kids can even assemble their own. It's really fun to make individual pizzas with the whole family.

---

1 (about 8") low-fat, whole wheat flour tortilla

2 tablespoons traditional barbecue sauce (7 grams carbohydrates or less per 2 tablespoons)

¾ ounce (about 3 tablespoons) goat cheese crumbles

3 tablespoons drained canned diced pineapple in juice, or drained pineapple rings in juice chopped into bite-sized pieces

1½ teaspoons finely chopped cilantro, or more to taste

Preheat the oven to 400°F.

Place the tortilla on a medium nonstick baking sheet. Bake for 2 to 4 minutes per side, or until crisp. If air bubbles form while baking, poke them with a fork, then use a spatula or oven mitt to carefully press the air out.

Remove from the oven and top evenly with the sauce, then the cheese, pineapple, and cilantro. Bake the pizza for 2 to 4 minutes longer, or until the cheese is completely melted. Slice into 8 wedges and serve.

Makes 1 serving

Per serving: 217 calories, 7 g protein, 35 g carbohydrates, 7 g fat (3 g saturated), 10 mg cholesterol, 2 g fiber, 484 mg sodium

MEATBALLS ON A STICK

These meatballs are great to layer on a platter for entertaining or just for family snacking. Serve skewered on toothpicks as suggested or divide them among larger skewers if you prefer.

1 cup Main Event Marinara Sauce (page 162) or other low-fat, low-sodium, low-sugar marinara sauce, reheated if necessary

New Favorite Meatballs (opposite page), reheated if necessary

Place the marinara sauce in a small bowl in the center of a serving platter. Skewer 2 meatballs onto each of 16 decorative toothpicks and arrange on the platter. Serve immediately.

Makes 4 servings

Per serving: 225 calories, 28 g protein, 17 g carbohydrates, 6 g fat (2 g saturated), 60 mg cholesterol, 3 g fiber, 330 mg sodium

Brady Vilcan, Season 6

After being away at the ranch, I came home and looked totally different to my kids. Now, when they watch me eat healthy food, they can see a concrete change in the way I look and feel. This is very encouraging to children because you're not just telling them to eat healthy, but you're actually showing them how to eat healthy!

NEW FAVORITE MEATBALLS

A lot of people opt for turkey or chicken meatballs and sausage, thinking that they're much leaner than beef. If you buy them pre-prepared, that does tend to be the case. But even the chicken and turkey meatballs and sausage you find at the grocery store or in restaurants derive at least 50% of their calories from fat and contain an insane amount of sodium. Yikes, right? That's why I make my own—they taste better and I can use real beef or real pork when I want. And if you and your family don't truly enjoy these meatballs more than the packaged chicken or turkey ones, I'll be shocked!

Olive oil spray

2   egg whites

½   cup quick-cooking oats

¼   cup fat-free milk

½   cup finely chopped fresh parsley

1   tablespoon dried minced onion

½   teaspoon dried oregano

½   teaspoon garlic powder

¼   teaspoon salt

⅛   teaspoon crushed red pepper flakes

1   pound 96% lean ground beef

Preheat the oven to 400°F. Lightly coat a large nonstick baking sheet with the olive oil spray.

In a medium bowl, using a fork, mix together the egg whites, oats, and milk until well combined. Add the parsley, onion, oregano, garlic powder, salt, and crushed red pepper flakes and mix until combined. Mix in the beef until well combined.

Make 32 uniform meatballs, each about 1¼" diameter (use a cookie scoop or 2 tablespoons for ease). Roll the balls with your hands and arrange, not touching, on the prepared baking sheet. Bake for 7 to 10 minutes, or until no longer pink inside.

Makes 4 (8-meatball) servings

Per serving: **194 calories, 26 g protein, 10 g carbohydrates, 5 g fat (2 g saturated), 60 mg cholesterol, 2 g fiber, 252 mg sodium**

HUMMUS-TUNA ENGLISH MUFFINS

This dish is great with any variety of hummus. So if you've purchased a different variety for another recipe in this book, or if you simply happen to have plain hummus in the fridge, don't spend extra money on the red pepper variety. Just use whatever you already have.

1 (6-ounce) can chunk light tuna in water, drained

¼ cup roasted red pepper–flavored hummus

2 light multigrain or whole wheat English muffins (8 grams fiber per muffin; I used Thomas'), halved and toasted

4 slices red onion

In a small bowl, mix the tuna with the hummus. Spoon evenly on the muffin halves (about 3 tablespoons each) and top each with a slice of red onion. Serve immediately.

Makes 4 servings

Per serving: 118 calories, 13 g protein, 15 g carbohydrates, 3 g fat (trace saturated), 12 mg cholesterol, 5 g fiber, 285 mg sodium

Curtis Bray, Season 5

It's not easy to go cold turkey and change your eating habits all at once. Give up one unhealthy food or activity each week and replace it with a healthy alternative, until you have gotten rid of all your old, unhealthy habits.

TUNA IN CELERY STICKS

This is one of my old standby snacks that is often enjoyed by a number of the contestants—both on and off campus. It's great for late-night munchies since it's salty, crunchy, and filling, yet contains no "bad" carbs—you definitely don't want those sitting in your stomach before bed. And it takes only seconds to throw together.

1 (6-ounce) can chunk light tuna in water, drained

1 tablespoon low-fat mayonnaise

4 medium (8") celery stalks, each cut in half

Garlic salt or salt-free lemon-pepper seasoning, to taste

In a small bowl, mix the tuna and mayonnaise with a fork until well combined. Divide evenly among the celery sticks. Season with garlic salt or lemon-pepper seasoning and serve.

Makes 4 servings

Per serving: 55 calories, 9 g protein, 3 g carbohydrates, less than 1 g fat (trace saturated), 11 mg cholesterol, 1 g fiber, 177 mg sodium

Amy Cremen, Season 6

Every night before you go to bed, prepare your lunch and snacks for the next day. Use snack-size bags for the correct portion sizes so you don't eat too much. This will help you avoid going through the drive-thru and frequenting the vending machine.

MELON TZATZIKI WITH RYKRISPS

If you're not familiar with it, tzatziki is a Greek yogurt dip that traditionally contains cucumbers; it is often served with pita bread in Greek restaurants. This twist on that popular favorite uses melon, which adds a touch of sweetness. I use RyKrisp crackers instead of pita, as they have much more fiber than most whole wheat pita circles. Feel free to swap in your favorite high-fiber crackers if you don't love RyKrisp as much as I do.

16 RyKrisp crackers

1 cup Melon Tzatziki
(opposite page)

Place 4 crackers on each of 4 serving plates. Top each cracker with 1 tablespoon of the tzatziki. Serve immediately.

Makes 4 servings

Per serving: 125 calories, 4 g protein, 27 g carbohydrates, trace fat (trace saturated), less than 1 mg cholesterol, 6 g fiber, 254 mg sodium

Ali Vincent, Season 5 Winner

I'm your snack girl! I love to snack! Successful snacking often depends on portability. Make them easy to take with you, like a piece of fruit with a few almonds. And string cheese—I always carry some around in my purse!

MELON TZATZIKI

Honeydew melons are in season from August to October, so if you buy one then, you'll save money and most likely get the sweetest fruit available. When choosing a honeydew, pick one that is heavy for its size and has a waxy (even slightly sticky) surface. If it's fuzzy, it's not ripe. It should also smell sweet and have a golden (not white) color.

1 cup fat-free plain yogurt

1 tablespoon finely chopped fresh mint

1 medium clove fresh garlic, minced

¼ teaspoon salt

¾ cup finely chopped honey-dew melon

In a medium bowl, combine the yogurt, mint, garlic, and salt and stir well to combine. Stir in the honeydew. Serve immediately or chill for up to 2 days.

Makes 6 (¼-cup) servings

Per serving: 25 calories, 2 g protein, 5 g carbohydrates, trace fat (trace saturated), less than 1 mg cholesterol, trace fiber, 124 mg sodium

From the Experts

Slash your grocery bill by supplementing your produce purchases with homegrown items. If you don't have space for a garden, you can at least grow your own herbs. Plant your favorites in small pots near the kitchen and take a snip or two as needed.

—Cheryl Forberg, RD, nutritionist for *The Biggest Loser*

EDAMAMMUS

This dip, which is like a hummus but made with edamame instead of chickpeas, is very versatile. You can serve it with your favorite veggies like carrots or celery and it's also great with toasted whole wheat pita triangles or your favorite high-fiber whole wheat crackers. To save money, buy the edamame frozen and cook it according to package directions.

8 ounces (about 1½ cups) cooked shelled edamame, cooled

2½ tablespoons freshly squeezed lemon juice

2 medium cloves fresh garlic, coarsely chopped

1 tablespoon fresh flat-leaf parsley, coarsely chopped

¼ teaspoon salt

1 teaspoon extra-virgin olive oil

3 tablespoons fat-free plain yogurt

In the bowl of a food processor fitted with the chopping blade, combine the edamame, lemon juice, garlic, parsley, and salt. Process until the mixture is paste-like and the edamame is finely chopped, scraping down the sides of the bowl as necessary. With the food processor on, slowly drizzle the olive oil through the top until well mixed. Add the yogurt and process just until combined. Serve immediately or refrigerate in an airtight container for up to 3 days.

Makes 5 (about ¼-cup) servings

Per serving: 66 calories, 5 g protein, 6 g carbohydrates, 3 g fat (trace saturated), trace cholesterol, 2 g fiber, 125 mg sodium

TEXAS CAVIAR

Trust me, this snack sounds a heck of a lot fancier and more expensive than it really is. You can serve it as a snack with baked chips or as a side dish to a meal. It is also really great for picnics.

Throughout the book I often suggest that you use "refrigerated, not jarred" salsas simply because the ingredients taste fresher and richer. It's rare that I go to the grocery store and can't find at least one brand of fresh salsa on sale (they also sell it in most club stores), so I always opt for that whenever possible.

---

1 (15-ounce) can 50% less-sodium black beans, rinsed and drained

1 (15-ounce) can 50% less-sodium whole kernel corn, rinsed and drained

¾ cup fresh salsa or pico de gallo (refrigerated, not jarred)

2 tablespoons chopped fresh cilantro

1½ teaspoons red wine vinegar

1 teaspoon cumin

Salt, to taste

Ground black pepper, to taste

Hot sauce, to taste

In a large glass or plastic mixing bowl or a large resealable plastic container, combine the beans, corn, salsa or pico de gallo, cilantro, vinegar, and cumin. Season with salt, pepper, and hot sauce. Cover and refrigerate at least 2 hours or overnight before serving.

Makes 6 (½-cup) servings

Per serving: 102 calories, 5 g protein, 25 g carbohydrates, trace fat (0 g saturated), 0 mg cholesterol, 4 g fiber, 269 sodium

From the Experts

Beans and legumes offer a myriad of health benefits as diverse as their varieties. Black beans, chickpeas, pintos—they're all excellent sources of fiber. They're also rich in folic acid, calcium, iron, potassium, zinc, and antioxidants. The complex carbohydrates they contain provide steady energy that lasts well beyond mealtime. A stellar source of protein, legumes may be the biggest money saver of all, as they cost a fraction of the price of most animal proteins.

—Cheryl Forberg, RD, nutritionist for *The Biggest Loser*

BLACK BEAN DIP

This dip is great with RyKrisps or your favorite veggies. With ⅛ teaspoon of the ground red pepper, it is quite mild and excellent for all ages. But if your family prefers spicy foods, you can use up to ½ teaspoon to make it nice and fiery.

1 (15-ounce) can 50% less-sodium black beans, drained

¼ cup chopped onion

¼ cup chopped green bell pepper

1 large clove fresh garlic, coarsely chopped

1 tablespoon lime juice, preferably freshly squeezed

1 tablespoon lemon juice, preferably freshly squeezed

½ teaspoon chili powder

½ teaspoon cumin

⅛ teaspoon ground red pepper, or more to taste

¼ teaspoon ground black pepper

⅛ teaspoon salt

⅓ cup diced fresh tomato

In the bowl of a large food processor fitted with a chopping blade, combine the black beans, onion, bell pepper, garlic, lime juice, lemon juice, chili powder, cumin, ground red pepper, black pepper, and salt. Pulse the ingredients until the mixture is paste-like and creamy but still slightly chunky, scraping down the sides of the bowl if necessary. Transfer the dip to a small, deep bowl and top with the tomatoes. Serve immediately or refrigerate in an airtight plastic container for up to 3 days.

Makes 7 (¼-cup) servings

Per serving: **42 calories, 3 g protein, 10 g carbohydrates, trace fat (trace saturated), 0 mg cholesterol, 3 g fiber, 169 mg sodium**

ENGLISH MUFFIN MELT

When shopping for tomatoes, try to find the least expensive variety. If beefsteak tomatoes are too pricey, try plum tomatoes instead. Just use four or eight ¼" slices plum tomatoes instead of the two larger slices.

When broiling, I always like to line my baking sheet with aluminum foil so the food doesn't stick and the intensity of the heat doesn't kill my pan. Plus, the cleanup is super easy. Individual broilers will vary in intensity, so always watch food closely when under the broiler to make sure it doesn't burn—it can happen fast.

1 light multigrain or whole wheat English muffin (8 grams fiber per muffin; I used Thomas'), halved and toasted

1 ounce (½ cup) finely shredded Cabot's 75% Light Cheddar Cheese, or your favorite low-fat Cheddar

2 (¼"-thick) slices beefsteak tomato

Preheat the broiler. Line a small, metal baking sheet with aluminum foil.

Place the muffin halves on the prepared baking sheet and sprinkle evenly with the cheese. Place 1 tomato slice on each muffin half over the cheese. Broil until the cheese bubbles and begins to brown in spots, 1 to 2 minutes. Serve immediately.

Makes 1 serving

Per serving: 168 calories, 15 g protein, 26 g carbohydrates, 4 g fat (2 g saturated), 12 mg cholesterol, 8 g fiber, 374 mg sodium

Matt Hoover, Season 2 Winner

Volume-wise, you can eat more healthy food than junk food for the same number of calories. Healthy food is much more filling.

KIWI-WATERMELON SALSA

In the summertime when watermelon is on sale, this salsa is a great alternative to traditional tomato salsa. It's refreshing and perfect for a picnic or barbecue. Serve with baked tortilla chips or toasted pita wedges.

While you should always be sure to wear gloves when working with jalapeños or wash your hands well afterwards (and keep the children clear of them), the good news is that the heat in jalapeños is known to naturally speed up your metabolism.

1 cup diced peeled kiwifruit (about 2 large or 3 small kiwis)

1 cup diced watermelon

⅓ cup finely chopped red onion

1 tablespoon finely chopped cilantro

2 teaspoons minced seeded jalapeño chile pepper (wear plastic gloves when handling)

2 teaspoons lime juice

Pinch of salt, or more to taste

In a medium glass or plastic mixing bowl, gently stir together the kiwi, watermelon, onion, cilantro, and jalapeño until well combined. Add the lime juice and salt and stir to combine. Serve immediately or refrigerate in an airtight container for up to 1 day.

Makes 9 (¼-cup) servings

Per serving: 23 calories, trace protein, 5 g carbohydrates, trace fat (trace saturated), 0 mg cholesterol, less than 1 g fiber, 17 mg sodium

ANTS ON AN OLIVE BRANCH

This recipe is a twist on the traditional snack favorite, Ants on a Log. If you can't find prepared hummus with black olives in the refrigerated section of your grocery store, just use ¼ cup of original flavored hummus and mix in 4 chopped or sliced kalamata olives. It will add only about 5 milligrams of sodium and 2 calories.

---

4 medium (8") celery stalks

¼ cup prepared hummus
   with black olives (I used
   the Athenos brand)

4 pitted kalamata olives,
   chopped

Place the celery sticks side by side on a plate. Spread 1 tablespoon of the hummus evenly into each piece of celery. Top each with one-fourth of the olives. Cut the celery sticks in half and serve.

Makes 4 servings

Per serving: 43 calories, less than 1 g protein, 5 g carbohydrates, 2 g fat (trace saturated), 0 mg cholesterol, 2 g fiber, 209 mg sodium

Heba Salama and Ed Brantley, Season 6

It's handy to have fresh cut fruit in bags, hard-boiled eggs, and small containers of yogurt ready to go—these are great power snacks to get you through an energy slump.

COTTAGE CHEESE WITH LEMON PEPPER

This is another satisfying snack to stave off the afternoon or evening hunger demons. It's nonfat, low-carb, high-protein, and very filling.

Many seasoning mixes are laden with salt. When you're buying lemon-pepper seasoning, make sure it doesn't have salt—look for "salt free" on the front or buy Mrs. Dash, which is always salt-free.

½ cup fat-free cottage cheese

¼ teaspoon salt-free lemon-pepper seasoning

Spoon the cottage cheese into a small, deep bowl and stir in the seasoning. Serve immediately.

Makes 1 serving

Per serving: 80 calories, 13 g protein, 7 g carbohydrates, 0 g fat, 5 mg cholesterol, 0 g fiber, 430 mg sodium

Budget Tips from The Biggest Loser

Become a semivegetarian to save on grocery bills. You can satisfy a lot of your daily protein needs with beans or egg whites. Eating two vegetarian meals a week will cut back on the cost of more expensive proteins like meat.

CRUNCHY BUGS ON A LOG

You've probably heard of Bugs on a Log . . . it's that snack that many of us enjoyed as children: celery sticks with peanut butter and raisins. Well, here it is again, but with a crunchy addition.

4 medium (8") celery stalks

2 tablespoons reduced-fat peanut butter

2 tablespoons raisins

8 teaspoons low-fat granola

Arrange the celery sticks on a plate. Spread ½ tablespoon peanut butter into each and top with ½ tablespoon raisins and 2 teaspoons granola. Cut the celery sticks in half crosswise and serve.

Makes 4 servings

Per serving: 87 calories, 3 g protein, 13 g carbohydrates, 3 g fat (less than 1 g saturated), 0 mg cholesterol, 2 g fiber, 132 mg sodium

Michelle Aguilar, Season 6

Any time you can get kids involved in the kitchen, make sure it's fun. Give the recipe a cool new name or let the kids name the dish.

TURKEY ON RYKRISPS

Admittedly, this is by far the most obvious recipe in the book. But it's such a favorite snack among so many of the contestants that I had to include it. There's something about deli turkey on really crispy crackers that is just so satisfying and filling. And with the fiber from the crackers and the protein from the turkey, you're bound to stave off unwanted munchies.

2 RyKrisp crackers

2 ounces Buffalo Turkey-Breast Roast (page 127), or other low-fat, low-sodium deli turkey, very thinly sliced

Place the crackers on a plate. Top each with 1 ounce of turkey and serve.

Makes 1 serving

Per serving: 114 calories, 14 g protein, 11 g carbohydrates, 1 g fat (trace saturated), 21 mg cholesterol, 3 g fiber, 145 mg sodium

Budget Tips from The Biggest Loser

Before you go to the grocery store, always take an inventory of what you may already have on your pantry shelves to avoid duplicate purchases. You don't want to end up with 10 jars of pickles!

TRAIL CORN

While traditional prepackaged trail mix usually contains wholesome ingredients, it also tends to have a lot of fat. This version has much less fat and a bit more fiber, yet is still likely to go un-traded when packed in the kids' lunches.

If you're not enjoying the trail corn immediately, it will stay freshest if you store the bags in a resealable plastic container.

---

4 cups air-popped popcorn

½ cup high-fiber, low-sugar cereal squares (I used Quaker Oatmeal Squares)

½ cup dried red fruit (such as dried cherries or dried cranberries)

2 tablespoons mini chocolate chips

In assembly line fashion, place 1 cup of popcorn into each of 4 sandwich-sized resealable plastic bags, followed by 2 tablespoons cereal, 2 tablespoons dried fruit, and ½ tablespoon chocolate chips. Shake each bag to distribute the ingredients evenly and seal. Eat immediately, or transfer the bags to an airtight container and store for up to 3 days.

Makes 4 (about 1¼-cup) servings

Per serving: 152 calories, 3 g protein, 29 g carbohydrates, 3 g fat (1 g saturated), 0 mg cholesterol, 4 g fiber, 37 mg sodium

COTTAGE CHEESE WITH MANDARIN ORANGES

I never used to be able to find unsweetened mandarin oranges, which are labeled "in juice." They more frequently said, "in slightly sweetened juice" or "in syrup." But now they are much easier to find, and since they don't contain processed sugars I've been enjoying them frequently. Here's a quick snack that the Biggest Loser families really enjoyed on campus.

½ cup fat-free cottage cheese

¼ cup drained mandarin oranges in juice

Spoon the cottage cheese into a small, deep bowl. Add the mandarin oranges and stir to combine. Serve immediately.

Makes 1 serving

Per serving: 103 calories, 13 g protein, 13 g carbohydrates, trace fat (0 g saturated), 5 mg cholesterol, trace fiber, 433 mg sodium

Bette-Sue Burklund, Season 5

Substitute fruit for candy if you have a sweet tooth. If I'm craving sour candy, I'll eat a tangerine instead. And the fiber in the fruit keeps your blood sugar steady.

BANANAS 'N' CREAM ENGLISH MUFFIN

High-fiber English muffins, bagels, and tortillas can be significantly more expensive than the white ones. But the good news is that they freeze really well—especially the English muffins—and once you toast them, you'll never know the difference. So when the healthier ones go on sale, stock your freezer.

½ light multigrain or whole wheat English muffin (8 grams fiber per muffin; I used Thomas'), toasted

1½ teaspoons light cream cheese

¼ medium banana, cut into ¼"-thick slices

Pinch of cinnamon

Place the toasted muffin half on a small plate and spread the cream cheese evenly over the top. Lay the banana slices over the cream cheese and sprinkle with cinnamon. Serve immediately.

Makes 1 serving

Per serving: 95 calories, 4 g protein, 20 g carbohydrates, 2 g fat (1 g saturated), 6 mg cholesterol, 5 g fiber, 113 mg sodium

Amy and Phillip Parham, Season 6

Freeze small containers of yogurt for a healthy snack. Our kids think it's like ice cream!

6

Dinner: More Than Just a Meal

Many of us come home each night to a dinner that meets at least one of the following descriptions: fast, frantic, tense, solitary, or unplanned. In the beginning, just about all cast members of *The Biggest Loser* arrive at the ranch having lived largely in the fast-food lane—Jerry Skeabeck of Season 6 was known to pick his dinner destination based on which fast-food restaurant had the shortest line. For other contestants, dinner was wolfed down while sitting alone in the car. Or eaten with their favorite dinner partner—television. Or given about as much thought as caf or decaf, diet or regular, fried or mashed.

Okay, folks, it's time to slow down and breathe, plan your meals, and enjoy them. If you make your shopping list and prep items when possible ahead of time (check out the tips throughout this book), you stand an even better chance of avoiding warp-speed dining.

Imagine sitting down to a table surrounded by family members and eating with awareness, enjoying every mouthful, tasting and savoring all the flavors and textures of the food you've prepared. You can think about what you're putting in your body, and you can pay attention to the people with whom you share your meal—and actually listen to what they have to say. The more you can do this, the healthier and happier your entire family is going to be.

As trainer Jillian Michaels points out, fueling your body with healthy food in the middle of the day will keep your metabolism on even keel. And you'll probably make better food choices at the end of the day, a danger zone for the lunch-deprived.

A lot of people think that dinner has to be a heavy, expensive meal. It doesn't. We've included an array of mix-and-match sides and entrées to fit every family's appetite and budget. If Italian food is a family favorite, why not try a healthy version of Baked Ziti, or Spirals and Meatballs? Or if Mexican is your thing, give our Shrimp Quesadilla or Enchilada Chicken a shot. Love Chinese takeout? How about Szechuan Beef and Broccoli or Hoisin-Glazed Pork Chops? You get our drift. The step from old behaviors to new ones isn't always as drastic and scary as it seems.

In fact, Season 5 winner Ali Vincent says she decides how light or substantial her dinner is going to be by what will follow it. Is she going to take a walk after dinner or go to a Pilates class? If so, she'll fuel accordingly. Is she going to relax after dinner, listen to music, read, or catch up with friends on the phone or online? Then she'll eat lighter. Make modifications based on your lifestyle and caloric needs.

Another important component of this slowed-down family dinner: Get the kids in the kitchen! No, you don't have to put a chef's knife in their little hands and ask them to chop away, but do ask them to set the table or set the oven timer or help measure or mix ingredients. Let them be a part of the preparation for this special time for the family to sit down together and appreciate a healthy meal they all helped create.

Don't be overwhelmed by the notion that you have to start eating every night with your family. We know that late nights at the office, soccer practice, and ballet recitals make that impossible sometimes. Maybe weekends will be an easier time to start bringing everyone together for a meal. But start somewhere; start here!

Poultry

MANDARIN ORANGE CHICKEN

When I started losing weight, I had to steer clear of my usual Chinese takeout; true, you can order steamed chicken and steamed veggies, blah, blah. To me, what's the point? After years of missing those rich flavors, I started incorporating the key ingredients back into my diet. Here I use mandarin oranges, lower-sodium soy sauce, chili garlic sauce, and even hot sesame oil. This is certainly not the traditional Chinese takeout that you'd find in that little white box, but I think you'll agree that my version rivals the old one any day.

3 tablespoons frozen orange juice concentrate, thawed

3 tablespoons lower-sodium soy sauce

1 tablespoon freshly minced garlic

1 tablespoon hot sesame oil

1 teaspoon chili garlic sauce or chili paste (found in the international section of most major grocery stores)

¾ cup canned unsweetened mandarin oranges in juice

6 (4-ounce) trimmed boneless, skinless chicken breasts

In a large, resealable plastic bag or container, mix the juice concentrate, soy sauce, garlic, oil, and chili sauce or chili paste. Gently stir in the oranges and their juice. Add the chicken, submerging it in marinade. Seal the bag or container and marinate in the refrigerator at least 6 hours or overnight, rotating once or twice.

Preheat the oven to 400°F. Transfer the chicken to an 11" × 7" glass baking or casserole dish (or the equivalent) in a single layer and pour the remaining marinade on top. Cover the dish with foil and bake for 25 to 30 minutes, or until the chicken is no longer pink inside.

Makes 6 servings

Per serving: **183 calories, 27 g protein, 7 g carbohydrates, 4 g fat (less than 1 g saturated), 66 mg cholesterol, trace fiber, 282 mg sodium**

ENCHILADA CHICKEN

I hadn't made enchiladas since the mid-80's until one of the Season 2 contestants mentioned that they were one of his favorite cheat foods. I was instantly inspired to try my hand at making enchiladas. It was such a hit, it ended up being featured on my show, Healthy Decadence. *Since then, I've tried all sorts of permutations, making it leaner and leaner. This version is the leanest yet, and since the dish is packed with lean protein, low in saturated fat, and virtually carb-free, our very own Dr. Dansinger is a fan, too!*

---

4 (4-ounce) trimmed bone-less, skinless chicken breasts

2 teaspoons salt-free Mexican or Southwest seasoning (I used Mrs. Dash Southwest Chipotle)

   Olive oil spray

4 tablespoons medium, mild, or hot enchilada sauce

2 ounces (1 cup) finely shredded Cabot's 75% Light Cheddar Cheese

2 tablespoons finely chopped fresh cilantro

Preheat the oven to 350°F.

Season each chicken breast evenly on all sides with the seasoning.

Place a large ovenproof nonstick skillet over high heat. When hot, lightly mist with the olive oil spray and add the chicken. Cook, turning once, for 1 to 2 minutes per side, or just until the chicken is golden brown on the outsides.

Remove the pan from the heat and top each chicken breast with 1 tablespoon of the enchilada sauce, followed by one-fourth of the cheese and one-fourth of the cilantro. Transfer the skillet to the oven and bake for 4 to 6 minutes, or until the chicken is no longer pink inside and the cheese is melted.

Makes 4 servings

Per serving: 162 calories, 31 g protein, 1 g carbohydrates, 3 g fat (1 g saturated), 71 mg cholesterol, trace fiber, 230 mg sodium

GOAT CHEESE–TOPPED TARRAGON CHICKEN

Goat cheese is becoming more and more popular, which is good news for our budgets. Not only can you find it at a good price at Trader Joe's (heck, Trader Joe's even has a light version), many major chain grocery stores are carrying it under their less expensive private labels (store brands). When it's on sale, check the date, then buy a couple of small containers—unlike many cheeses, it often stays good for months if the package remains sealed.

4   **(4-ounce) trimmed bone-less, skinless chicken breasts**

     Olive oil in a sprayer (not store-bought spray that contains propellant)

1¼   **teaspoons dried tarragon**

⅛   **teaspoon salt, or more to taste**

     Ground black pepper, to taste

1   **ounce (about ¼ cup) goat cheese crumbles**

Preheat the oven to 350°F.

Lightly mist the chicken breasts with olive oil and season evenly all over with the tarragon, salt, and pepper.

Place a large ovenproof nonstick skillet over high heat. When hot, lightly mist with olive oil. Add the chicken and cook, turning once, for 1 to 2 minutes per side, or until golden brown on the outsides. Transfer the skillet to the oven and bake for 4 minutes. Top each breast with one-fourth of the goat cheese. Continue baking for 2 to 3 minutes, or until the cheese is slightly melted, the chicken is no longer pink, and juices run clear.

Makes 4 servings

Per serving: 146 calories, 28 g protein, trace carbohydrates, 3 g fat (1g saturated), 69 mg cholesterol, trace fiber, 173 mg sodium

Vicky Vilcan, Season 6

Ask the kids to help you measure out portions when you're cooking. It teaches them portion control and makes them feel useful.

SWEET AND SOUR CHICKEN STIR-FRY

Though this dish does have some sugar and some sodium, it is a far cry from the nutritional suicide you face in most traditional Chinese restaurants. It's a good idea to cut the chicken into small, bite-sized pieces so you can really taste the sauce. Also, make sure you add the sauce after the chicken is removed from the pan. If you add the sauce to the hot pan, the sauce will cook and get stuck to the bottom of the pan—and you won't get to enjoy it.

1 tablespoon cornstarch

1 teaspoon garlic powder

¼ teaspoon salt

Ground black pepper, to taste

1 pound trimmed boneless, skinless chicken breasts, cut into bite-sized cubes

1 tablespoon toasted sesame oil

1 cup ½"-wide strips onion (about 1" long)

1 cup ½"-wide strips green bell pepper (about 1" long)

2 tablespoons freshly minced garlic

¼ cup bottled sweet and sour stir-fry sauce (I used La Choy)

In a large bowl, combine the cornstarch, garlic powder, salt, and pepper and mix well. Add the chicken and toss until the chicken pieces are thoroughly coated.

Place a large nonstick skillet or nonstick wok over high heat. When hot, add 1 teaspoon sesame oil, onion, pepper, and garlic. Cook, stirring, until the garlic softens and the vegetables are crisp-tender, 2 to 4 minutes. Be careful not to overcook or the garlic may burn. Transfer the vegetables to a large bowl and cover to keep warm.

Return the pan to high heat and add another teaspoon sesame oil and half the chicken in a single layer. Cook until the pieces are lightly browned on the bottom. Flip the pieces and continue cooking until chicken is no longer pink and juices run clear, 4 to 6 minutes. Add the cooked chicken to the bowl with the vegetables. Return the pan to high heat, add the remaining oil, and cook the remaining chicken.

Return the vegetables and chicken to the pan to reheat if necessary. Transfer to a medium serving bowl, add the sauce, and mix until well combined. Divide the stir-fry among 4 serving bowls and serve.

Makes 4 servings

Per serving: 223 calories, 27 g protein, 16 g carbohydrates, 5 g fat (less than 1 g saturated), 66 mg cholesterol, 1 g fiber, 283 mg sodium

GRILLED CHICKEN PARMESAN

As a kid, I was obsessed with chicken Parmesan—it didn't matter if we were going out for fast food or fine dining, I was ordering it. The turning point in my weight loss journey was when I heard that if you just cut 100 calories from your diet per day, on average, you'll lose 10 pounds in a year. It sounded too good to be true, but I tried it . . . and this was the first dish I tried it with, and therefore the dish that led to my career. At the time, my cooking skills were pretty basic, but now, after years of substitutions (and obsessing over every ingredient), I can make dozens of simple, crave-busting dishes. Serve with a side of whole wheat pasta and/or a large green salad.

4 (4-ounce) trimmed boneless, skinless chicken breasts

Olive oil in a sprayer (not store-bought spray that contains propellant)

Salt, to taste

Ground black pepper, to taste

½ cup Main Event Marinara Sauce (page 162) or other low-fat, low-sodium, low-sugar marinara sauce, or more to taste

6 tablespoons finely shredded low-fat mozzarella cheese

2 teaspoons grated reduced-fat Parmesan cheese

Preheat the oven to 350°F. Preheat a grill to high heat.

Lightly mist both sides of the chicken with olive oil and season with salt and pepper. Grill the chicken, turning once, for 3 to 5 minutes per side, or until it is no longer pink inside and juices run clear. Transfer to a baking dish.

Heat the sauce on low in the microwave until warm. Top each breast with 2 tablespoons marinara sauce, followed by 1½ tablespoons mozzarella, and ½ teaspoon Parmesan. Bake the chicken for 3 to 5 minutes, or just until the cheese is melted.

Makes 4 servings

Per serving: 169 calories, 29 g protein, 5 g carbohydrates, 3 g fat (less than 1 g saturated), 70 mg cholesterol, 1 g fiber, 210 mg sodium

PARTY CHICKEN KEBABS

Every year, I go out on my friend Chris's boat for the Fourth of July. He always says that he'll supply the boat if I supply the food and the cute girls. No problem: It's not like there's ever a shortage of cute girls in L.A. or a shortage of food around me. I pack up tons of healthy appetizers and picnic-type foods along with these Mediterranean-inspired kebabs. Though we're far from the Mediterranean in California, it never hurts to eat food so good that you feel like you're in the Greek Isles.

- ¼ cup freshly squeezed lemon juice
- 3½ tablespoons freshly minced garlic
- 2 tablespoons extra-virgin olive oil
- 2 tablespoons finely chopped fresh rosemary
- 1½ teaspoons finely chopped fresh sage
- 1½ tablespoons honey
- 1½ teaspoons coarsely ground black pepper
- ¾ teaspoon salt
- 1 pound trimmed boneless, skinless chicken breasts, cut into 1½" cubes

In a small bowl, whisk together the lemon juice, garlic, olive oil, rosemary, sage, honey, pepper, and salt. Place the chicken in a resealable plastic container, add the marinade, and toss. Cover and marinate in the refrigerator for at least 6 hours or overnight, turning the chicken at least once.

Preheat a grill to high. Soak 4 wooden skewers in water for at least 30 minutes (or have metal skewers ready).

Thread the chicken cubes onto the 4 skewers. Place the kebabs on the grill and reduce the heat to low. Grill for 2 minutes and rotate a quarter-turn. Continue to grill, turning, for 1 to 2 minutes per side, or until the chicken is no longer pink inside and juices run clear.

Makes 4 servings

Per serving: 160 calories, 26 g protein, 4 g carbohydrates, 4 g fat (less than 1 g saturated), 66 mg cholesterol, trace fiber, 220 mg sodium

THYME FRIED CHICKEN

If you have trouble finding bone-in chicken breasts that are only 6 or 7 ounces, don't worry. Simply ask the butcher at your local grocery store to cut much larger ones in half or to trim some that are slightly larger. More often than not, they'll cut them for free. You can use any remaining pieces for another recipe.

4 small (6- to 7-ounce) bone-in chicken breasts, trimmed of skin and visible fat

1¼ cups buttermilk

Olive oil in a sprayer (not store-bought spray that contains propellant)

2 teaspoons dry mustard

1 teaspoon dried thyme

1 teaspoon garlic powder

¼ teaspoon salt, plus more to taste

½ teaspoon ground black pepper

1 cup whole wheat panko (Japanese bread crumbs; I used Ian's)

Combine the chicken breasts and buttermilk in a large resealable plastic bag or container. Turn the breasts so they are completely coated and seal the bag or container. Marinate in the refrigerator at least 6 hours or overnight, turning the breasts once or twice.

Preheat the oven to 450°F. Lightly mist a medium nonstick baking sheet with olive oil.

In a small bowl, mix the mustard, thyme, garlic powder, ¼ teaspoon of the salt, and the black pepper. Place the panko in a medium shallow bowl. Remove one chicken breast from the buttermilk and let any excess buttermilk drip off. Sprinkle the breast evenly all over with about one-fourth of the thyme mixture. Dip the breast in the panko, rotating to cover completely. Repeat with the remaining chicken.

Place the breaded breasts face down (ribs up) on the prepared sheet so they do not touch and lightly spray the tops with olive oil. Bake for 10 minutes. Being careful not to remove any breading, turn the breasts and lightly spray with olive oil. Bake for 10 to 15 minutes longer, or until the breading is crispy and the chicken is no longer pink inside. Serve immediately or refrigerate for up to 2 days to serve cold.

Makes 4 servings

Per serving: 194 calories, 26 g protein, 16 g carbohydrates, 3 g fat (trace saturated), 55 mg cholesterol, 2 g fiber, 397 mg sodium

CHICKEN WITH SAGE GRAVY

There are plenty of jarred and canned gravies in grocery stores now that are quite low in fat and calories. When you incorporate a fresh herb, you can make this convenient staple taste a bit more homemade. Here, I use fresh sage to make a rich, memorable dish. If you have a local farmers' market (even most small towns now do), it's worth checking out. Herbs from local farms tend to be a fraction of the cost compared to what you'd pay at the grocery store.

4 (4-ounce) trimmed boneless, skinless chicken breasts

1 teaspoon extra-virgin olive oil

1 tablespoon minced fresh sage

Salt, to taste

Ground black pepper, to taste

½ cup canned fat-free chicken gravy

Rub the chicken breasts with the olive oil and season all over with the sage, salt, and pepper.

Place a medium nonstick skillet over high heat. When hot, add the chicken and cook for 1 to 2 minutes per side, or until golden brown on the outside. Add the gravy and reduce the heat to low. Cover and simmer for 7 to 9 minutes, or until the chicken is no longer pink. Serve immediately.

Makes 4 servings

Per serving: 146 calories, 27 g protein, 2 g carbohydrate, 3 g fat (less than 1 g saturated), 68 mg cholesterol, 0 g fiber, 200 mg sodium

Biggest Loser Trainer Tip: Bob Harper

Fresh herbs are all about flavor—adding them to food will give you a whole new outlook. For example, add a little rosemary to your chicken and you're going to have a whole new taste!

BUFFALO CHICKEN–BLUE CHEESE MEAT LOAF

I don't think a single season of The Biggest Loser *has gone by without some of the contestants complaining that they miss their chicken wings. At first I created a lighter buffalo wing plate with the typical wings, carrot sticks, celery sticks, and blue cheese dressing—just like you'd get at the local bar. But then I realized that the components would be excellent if turned into a meat loaf. So here it is. Just be cautious of wing sauces with too much sodium. The brands with less sodium often have a bit more fat, but since you tend to use such a small amount they're generally a better choice. And look for a thick, all-natural sauce, but definitely not a thin one like Tabasco; I like to use Wing-Time Hot Buffalo Wing Sauce.*

Olive oil spray

⅔ cup old-fashioned oats

½ cup fat-free milk

2½ tablespoons buffalo wing sauce, or more to taste

1 pound extra-lean ground chicken breast

½ cup finely chopped celery

¼ cup shredded carrot

¼ cup finely chopped sweet onion

2 large egg whites, lightly beaten

¼ teaspoon salt

2 ounces (about ½ cup) crumbled reduced-fat blue cheese

Preheat the oven to 350°F. Lightly mist a 9" × 5" × 3" (slightly smaller is OK) nonstick loaf pan with the olive oil spray.

Combine the oats and milk in a medium mixing bowl and stir to mix. Let stand for 3 minutes, or until the oats begin to soften. Stir in the wing sauce until well mixed. Add the chicken, celery, carrot, onion, egg whites, and salt. With a fork or clean hands, mix the ingredients well. Add the blue cheese and gently mix to combine.

Transfer the mixture to the prepared pan and spread so that the top is flat. Bake for 35 to 40 minutes, or until the chicken is completely cooked through and no longer pink. Cut into 8 slices and serve immediately.

Makes 4 servings

Per serving: 263 calories, 35 g protein, 14 g carbohydrates, 6 g fat (2 g saturated), 74 mg cholesterol, 2 g fiber, 485 mg sodium

BBQ-BACON MEAT LOAF

Bread crumbs are traditionally used in meat loaf and meatballs to add moisture to the finished dish and, sometimes, even to add bulk to stretch the meat for your dollar. I often use oatmeal instead as it will do the trick to create moist and delicious dishes while adding fiber—it's not just a bunch of white flour. I don't add too much because I still want the dishes to be predominantly protein-based, but it's very important to add some, especially with leaner meat like chicken and turkey breast. With the right recipe, turkey and chicken loaves can taste just as fattening as their beef counterparts! Got leftovers? Use them to make my BBQ-Bacon Meat Loaf Sandwich (page 62).

Olive oil spray

1 cup chopped red onion

4 slices extra-lean turkey bacon, chopped

⅔ cup old-fashioned oats

½ cup fat-free milk

1 pound extra-lean ground chicken breast

2 large egg whites, lightly beaten

1 clove fresh garlic, minced

1 teaspoon Worcestershire sauce

⅛ teaspoon salt

⅓ cup barbecue sauce (7 grams carbohydrates or less per 2 tablespoons)

Preheat the oven 350°F. Lightly mist a 9" × 5" × 3" nonstick loaf pan with the olive oil spray.

Place a medium nonstick skillet over medium-high heat. Lightly mist the pan with spray and add the onion and bacon. Cook, stirring, for 6 to 8 minutes, or until the onion is tender and just barely starting to brown and the bacon is crisped. Remove the pan from the heat and allow the mixture to cool.

Combine the oats and milk in a medium mixing bowl and stir to mix. Let the mixture stand for 3 minutes, or until the oats begin to soften. Add the cooled onion and bacon mixture, the chicken, egg whites, garlic, Worcestershire sauce, and salt. With a fork or clean hands, mix the ingredients until well combined.

Transfer the mixture to the prepared pan and spread so the top is flat. Spread the barbecue sauce evenly over the top. Bake for 35 to 40 minutes, or until the chicken is completely cooked through and no longer pink. Let the loaf sit for 10 minutes before cutting into 8 slices to serve.

Makes 4 servings

Per serving: 258 calories, 35 g protein, 20 g carbohydrates, 3 g fat (trace saturated), 76 mg cholesterol, 2 g fiber, 529 mg sodium

SIMPLE GRILLED CHICKEN

This chicken is perfect to keep on hand for munching or for using in other dishes like quesadillas, salads, sandwiches, and more. If you buy your chicken in bulk and cook extra, you'll save time and money when hunger and dinnertime strikes.

4 (4-ounce) trimmed bone-less, skinless chicken breasts

Olive oil in a sprayer (not store-bought spray that contains propellant)

2 teaspoons salt-free garlic and herb seasoning (I used Mrs. Dash)

Salt, to taste

Preheat a grill to high heat.

Lightly mist the chicken breasts with olive oil. Rub the seasoning evenly all over each breast and lightly season with salt. Grill for 3 to 5 minutes per side, or until the chicken is no longer pink and juices run clear. Serve immediately or store in an airtight plastic container in the refrigerator for up to 3 days.

Makes 4 servings

Per serving: 127 calories, 26 g protein, 0 g carbohydrates, 2 g fat (trace saturated), 66 mg cholesterol, 0 g fiber, 74 mg sodium

Amy and Phillip Parham, Season 6

We cook a lot of chicken at once and store it in resealable plastic bags so we have it on hand to whip up a quick dinner. We've learned to use mustard, salsa, and spices other than salt for seasonings. (I never realized how much sodium can affect weight loss!) Also, we steam and store veggies so we'll have them ready all the time.

BUFFALO TURKEY-BREAST ROAST

If you have trouble finding a boneless turkey breast roast, look for a bone-in version that weighs about 3 pounds (after deboning, without using the tenderloin, it should come out to about 1½ pounds). If you don't want to debone the roast yourself, just ask your butcher. If you find a turkey breast slightly smaller than 3 pounds, you can use the deboned roast with the tenderloin still attached to get 1½ pounds of turkey.

If you want turkey that is mild in flavor and perfect for sandwiches, use 1 tablespoon of wing sauce. But if you're going to eat this on its own, use more sauce for that buffalo wing flavor and heat.

Olive oil spray

¼ teaspoon garlic powder

¼ teaspoon salt

¼ teaspoon ground black pepper

1½ pounds trimmed boneless, skinless turkey breast roast

1 teaspoon extra-virgin olive oil

1 to 2 tablespoons buffalo wing sauce (Look for a thick, all-natural sauce, but definitely not a thin one like Tabasco; I like to use Wing-Time Hot Buffalo Wing Sauce.)

¼ cup water

Preheat the oven to 350°F. Lightly mist an 8" × 8" glass baking dish or nonstick baking pan with the olive oil spray.

In a small bowl, combine the garlic powder, salt, and pepper. Place the roast on a cutting board. With a fork, pierce each side (top and bottom) deeply about 25 times. Drizzle on the oil and rub to coat evenly on both sides. Sprinkle with the garlic powder mixture and rub it in to evenly coat both sides.

With the smooth side of the breast down, drizzle with half of the wing sauce, rubbing to coat. Place the turkey, smooth side up, in the prepared pan. Rub the buffalo sauce over the smooth side of the breast. Pour the water into the pan, taking care not to pour it over the turkey.

Roast for 35 to 40 minutes, or until a thermometer inserted in the thickest portion registers 160°F. and the juices run clear. Tent the roast loosely with foil and let stand for 10 minutes (the temperature should increase to 170°F.). Place the turkey on a clean cutting board and carve against the grain into thin slices. Serve immediately or refrigerate in an airtight plastic container for up to 3 days.

Makes 5 (about 4-ounce) servings

Per serving: 158 calories, 34 g protein, trace carbohydrates, 3 g fat (trace saturated), 54 mg cholesterol, trace fiber, 198 mg sodium

GRILLED TURKEY CUTLETS WITH SALSA

I love grilling turkey cutlets because they cook so quickly and much more evenly than larger cuts of turkey. This dish has been a staple in my house for years. And since it can be made with numerous varieties of salsa, you're not likely to tire of it quickly.

1 teaspoon extra-virgin olive oil

1 pound boneless, skinless turkey cutlets

⅛ to ¼ teaspoon seasoned salt, to taste

½ teaspoon salt-free, extra-spicy seasoning (I used Mrs. Dash Extra Spicy)

6 tablespoons fresh salsa (refrigerated, not jarred), any variety

Preheat a grill to high heat.

Rub the oil all over the cutlets and season evenly with the seasoned salt and seasoning. Grill about 1 minute per side, or until no longer pink inside. Transfer the cutlets to a platter, top with the salsa, and serve.

Makes 4 servings

Per serving: 134 calories, 28 g protein, 2 g carbohydrates, 2 g fat (trace saturated), 45 mg cholesterol, 0 g fiber, 155 mg sodium

Biggest Loser Online Club: Tari Pierce, Season 6

My husband is a Texan through and through. He loves his steak and potatoes. So, to save a few bucks and keep the man happy at the same time, I have substituted some of his steak days with turkey kielbasa days. It's much cheaper and healthier, and he doesn't know the difference!

Change your life today! Log on to www.biggestloserclub.com and get started

SWEDISH MEATBALLS

This recipe is a remake of an authentic meatball recipe shared with me by a Swedish immigrant. One serving saves you 171 calories and 20 grams of fat compared to a same-sized serving of the original. Just be sure to use a whole wheat bread that is on the fluffier side and not too grainy.

2   slices fluffy whole wheat bread (about 70 calories per slice)

⅓   cup fat-free milk

1   large egg white

½   cup finely chopped yellow onion

2   tablespoons prepared horseradish

½   teaspoon sugar

1¾   teaspoons ground allspice

¼   teaspoon salt

¼   teaspoon ground black pepper

1   pound extra-lean ground turkey

3   cups reduced-sodium, fat-free chicken broth

     Olive oil spray

¾   cup light sour cream

In a mixing bowl, soak the bread in the milk until it's absorbed. Tear the soggy bread into small pieces. Add the egg white, onion, 1 tablespoon horseradish, the sugar, ¼ teaspoon allspice, the salt, and pepper. Mix, then add the turkey, mixing just until combined.

In a 2- or 2½-quart soup pot, bring the broth and 1 teaspoon of the allspice to a full rolling boil over high heat.

Roll the turkey mixture into 1½" meatballs. Boil half the meatballs in the broth for 3 to 7 minutes, or until they rise to the surface and are no longer pink inside. Transfer them to a serving bowl.

Heat a large nonstick skillet to high heat. When hot, mist with spray. Add the meatballs, working in batches if necessary and cook, stirring occasionally, until lightly browned, 2 to 4 minutes. Return the meatballs to the serving bowl and cover to keep warm.

Strain the broth through a sieve into a bowl. Measure out ¾ cup and add to the skillet. Place over high heat and boil until reduced by half, 4 to 6 minutes. Whisk in the sour cream, remaining 1 tablespoon horseradish, and remaining ½ teaspoon allspice. The mixture should have the consistency of a smooth, creamy gravy. If it does not, add a bit more broth to make it thinner or continue to boil, stirring, until it reduces and thickens. Pour the sauce over the meatballs and serve hot.

Makes 4 (10-meatball) servings

Per serving: 244 calories, 35 g protein, 18 g carbohydrates, 5 g fat (2 g saturated), 60 mg cholesterol, 2 g fiber, 698 mg sodium

BENCH PRESS BELL PEPPERS

This dish is great using any color bell peppers. I prefer red, but when shopping on a budget and the red ones aren't on sale, I'll happily go for the green to save some green. You may notice I often call for "freshly minced garlic." I much, much, much prefer it over the preminced stuff you buy in jars. That garlic is usually packed in citric acid, which alters the taste. If you can, stick to the fresh stuff and do the chopping yourself.

2 large green bell peppers

Olive oil spray

1 pound extra-lean ground turkey breast

3 tablespoons freshly minced garlic

2 cups cooked brown rice

2 large egg whites, lightly beaten

¼ cup chopped fresh mint

3 ounces reduced-fat feta cheese crumbles

Pinch of salt

Preheat the oven to 375°F. Carefully pull the stems off the peppers (without breaking the peppers). Cut the peppers in half from top to bottom and remove the cores and seeds.

Fill a large pot two-thirds with water and bring to a boil over high heat. Add the peppers and boil for 5 minutes. Drain and place on a cutting board or flat work surface.

Meanwhile, place a large nonstick skillet over medium-high heat. When hot, lightly mist with the olive oil spray. Add the turkey and garlic and cook, breaking the turkey into bite-sized chunks, until no longer pink, 3 to 5 minutes. Transfer to a medium bowl and add the rice, egg whites, mint, feta, and salt. Mix well, then carefully (the mixture will be a bit hot) spoon one-fourth of the mixture into each pepper half, forming a mound.

Place the peppers, stuffed side up, in an 8" × 8" glass or ceramic baking dish. Add enough water to come about ¼" up the sides. Bake for 20 minutes, or until the peppers are tender, the filling is hot, and a very light crust starts to form on the top.

Makes 4 servings

Per serving: 311 calories, 38 g protein, 30 g carbohydrates, 5 g fat (2 g saturated), 51 mg cholesterol, 4 g fiber, 429 mg sodium

FAMILY-SIZED CHICKEN CHEESE STEAK

The key to creating perfectly cooked chicken for this sandwich is to make sure the pan is hot and large enough for the chicken to lie flat when it cooks. It's particularly important when you're cooking without a lot of fat. A cold pan or a heap of chicken will prevent the meat from getting that great browned flavor and color. So turn up the heat like we do in my hometown of Philly!

---

1 (8-ounce) whole wheat or multigrain baguette

1 pound trimmed boneless, skinless chicken breasts

Olive oil spray

1 cup slivered white onion

Salt, to taste

Ground black pepper, to taste

4 (¾-ounce) slices light 2% yellow American cheese, each cut in half crosswise

¼ cup no-salt-added ketchup (I used Heinz)

3 tablespoons sliced, pickled hot chile peppers or pepperoncini, or to taste

Preheat the oven to 400°F. Cut a piece of aluminum foil a couple of inches longer than the baguette. Cut the baguette as you would cut a roll to make a sandwich, then wrap it in the foil.

Shave the chicken by holding a very sharp knife at a 45° angle and cutting slivers from the breasts, basically tearing the chicken until it's all shaved—it should be much more finely cut than if it were simply sliced. Place the baguette in the oven to warm, about 10 minutes.

Place a large nonstick skillet over medium-high heat. When hot, lightly mist with spray. Add the onion and cook, stirring, until tender, 6 to 9 minutes. Transfer to a large bowl and cover to keep warm.

Return the pan to high heat. When hot, mist again with the spray and add half of the chicken. Season with salt and pepper. Cook, pulling apart the chicken shavings with 2 spatulas, until no longer pink and lightly browned in places, about 2 minutes. Transfer to the bowl with the onion. Repeat with the remaining chicken. Reduce the heat to low and return all the chicken and the onion to the pan until warmed.

Unwrap the baguette. Add the cheese slices, evenly, side by side. Add the chicken mixture, packing it into the sandwich. Top with the ketchup, then the peppers. Cut crosswise into 4 equal sandwiches and serve.

Makes 4 servings

Per serving: 340 calories, 36 g protein, 34 g carbohydrates, 6 g fat (2 g saturated), 76 mg cholesterol, 3 g fiber, 571 mg sodium

JAM-PACKED CHICKEN SOFT TACOS

You'll notice that I use ground chicken breast a lot throughout this book. I find it to be a better substitute for beef than ground turkey. The moisture content in ground chicken is similar to that of ground beef; turkey is drier. Also, turkey has a stronger, more distinct flavor. Ground chicken can often be seasoned to taste more like beef. Plus, if the ground chicken isn't on sale or you can't find the extra-lean kind, you can always save money by having your butcher grind it for you. Most will do it at no charge.

4 (7½") low-fat, low-carb multigrain or whole wheat tortillas

   Olive oil spray

1 pound extra-lean ground chicken breast

1 tablespoon + 1 teaspoon salt-free Mexican seasoning (I used Mrs. Dash Southwest Chipotle)

8 teaspoons fat-free sour cream

4 ounces (2 cups) finely shredded Cabot's 75% Light Cheddar Cheese

1 cup shredded romaine lettuce

1 cup chopped seeded tomatoes

4 tablespoons red taco sauce, or to taste

Preheat the oven to 400°F. Stack the tortillas on a large piece of foil and roll into a tube to encase the tortillas. Seal the ends. Place the tortillas in the oven for about 5 minutes, or until warm.

Place a large nonstick skillet over medium-high heat. When hot, mist with the olive oil spray. Add the chicken and sprinkle with the seasoning. Cook, breaking the chicken into large chunks, until no longer pink. Remove from the heat.

Unroll the warmed tortillas. Place a tortilla on a plate and spread 2 teaspoons of the sour cream in a 3"-wide strip down the center. Spoon one-fourth of the chicken over the sour cream, followed by one-fourth of the cheese, ¼ cup of the lettuce, ¼ cup of the tomatoes, and 1 tablespoon of the taco sauce. Fold the tortilla in half to form a taco. Repeat with the remaining ingredients and serve.

Makes 4 servings

Per serving: 316 calories, 43 g protein, 18 g carbohydrates, 7 g fat (2 g saturated), 77 mg cholesterol, 9 g fiber, 462 mg sodium

"STUFFED CABBAGE" STRATA

I grew up eating a version of this dish that my mom called Cabbage Casserole. I really wanted to include my version in this book because it is one of those surprisingly tasty dishes that is perfect for people who, like me, love to eat large portions but want to stay healthy. One serving is a huge amount of food, particularly for the amount of fat and calories.

Please don't substitute ground turkey here. It won't complement the dish. Though I actually prefer chicken in this dish, you can also use 96% lean ground beef.

Olive oil spray

8 slices center-cut bacon, cut into 2" pieces

1¼ cups minced yellow onions

1 cup uncooked instant brown rice (or instant white rice in a pinch)

6 cups shredded green cabbage

1½ pounds extra-lean ground chicken breast

½ teaspoon salt

¼ teaspoon ground black pepper

2 (8-ounce) cans no-salt-added tomato sauce

¾ cup water

Hot sauce, to taste (optional)

Preheat the oven to 400°F. Lightly spray an 8" × 8" (at least 2¼" deep) ovenproof glass or ceramic casserole or baking dish with the olive oil spray. Line a dinner plate with a paper towel.

Place a large nonstick skillet over medium-high heat. Add the bacon and cook for 4 to 6 minutes per side, or until the bacon is cooked and starting to crisp on the edges. Transfer the bacon to the lined plate. Discard all but 1 tablespoon of the bacon fat from the skillet.

Add the onions and rice to the skillet and place over medium heat. Cook in the bacon fat, stirring, until the onions are tender and the rice is just starting to brown, 3 to 5 minutes.

Spread 3 cups of the cabbage in an even layer on the bottom of the prepared baking dish. Top with the rice mixture, forming an even layer.

Add the chicken, salt, and pepper to the skillet and place over medium-high heat. Cook the chicken, breaking it up with a wooden spoon, but leaving some large chunks, until no longer pink, 3 to 5 minutes. With a slotted spoon, transfer the chicken to the casserole dish to form another even layer. Spread the remaining 3 cups cabbage over the chicken.

Discard any liquid from the skillet and add the tomato sauce and water. Turn the heat to high and bring to a boil. With a ladle or large spoon, carefully spoon the sauce evenly over the casserole, being sure that the dish doesn't overflow. Lay the bacon pieces evenly on top of the cabbage.

Cover the dish with aluminum foil and bake for 45 minutes. Uncover and bake 10 minutes longer, or until the cabbage and rice are tender and the strata is heated through. Let stand 5 minutes to set. Cut into 6 equal pieces and serve with hot sauce on the side, if desired.

Makes 6 servings

Per serving: 271 calories, 32 g protein, 25 g carbohydrates, 5 g fat (2 g saturated), 75 mg cholesterol, 5 g fiber, 462 mg sodium

Fish and Seafood

LOSERS' FISH TACOS

You'll notice throughout the book, I include both salt-free seasoning and salt in some recipes. Though this may seem odd at first glance, there's a method to this healthy-cooking madness. If you look at the ingredient list of most seasonings that do contain salt, you'll see that it's first on the list, meaning there's more salt than any other ingredient. That often means it's too much salt to flavor a dish properly without oversalting. So I use salt-free seasoning and then just add a hint of salt. It's a great trick to help get the seasoning you want and control the salt.

---

8   taco-sized (5½") corn tortillas

1   pound Alaskan pollack (mahimahi or monkfish are great too), cut into 1" pieces

2   tablespoons salt-free Mexican seasoning (I used Mrs. Dash Southwest Chipotle)

Salt, to taste

Olive oil spray

2   cups slightly drained Coleslaw with Orange-Cilantro Vinaigrette (page 181)

½   cup fresh pico de gallo or fresh salsa (refrigerated, not jarred), drained if watery

2   tablespoons chopped fresh cilantro, or more to taste

Stack the tortillas and wrap in a clean, damp, lint-free dish towel (or damp paper towels).

Season the fish evenly with the seasoning and salt.

Place a large nonstick skillet over medium-high heat. When hot, lightly mist with the olive oil spray. Working in batches if necessary, add the fish pieces in a single layer. Cook, turning occasionally, for 3 to 5 minutes, or until the fish flakes easily in the center and is lightly browned.

Meanwhile, microwave the stack of tortillas on low until warmed, 15 to 30 seconds.

Transfer 2 tortillas to each of 4 dinner plates, placing the tortillas side by side on each plate. Divide the fish evenly among the tortillas, placing it in a strip down the center. Top with the coleslaw, then the salsa. Sprinkle with the cilantro, fold the tortillas to form tacos, and serve.

Makes 4 servings

Per serving: 281 calories, 27 g protein, 34 g carbohydrates, 5 g fat (less than 1 g saturated), 82 mg cholesterol, 6 g fiber, 216 mg sodium

ROASTED TILAPIA WITH FIRE-ROASTED TOMATOES AND OLIVES

If you haven't seen them, fire-roasted tomatoes are newly emerging in popularity—you'll now find them with the other canned tomatoes in most major grocery stores. I love them because they are packed with flavor yet have no more fat or calories than traditional diced tomatoes.

⅔ cup canned fire-roasted diced tomatoes

12 small green olives with pimientos (sometimes called manzillas), cut into quarters

1 tablespoon + 1 teaspoon minced onion

1 teaspoon freshly crushed or minced garlic

1 pound tilapia fillets

Olive oil in a sprayer (not store-bought spray that contains propellant)

Salt, to taste

Ground black pepper, to taste

Preheat the oven to 400°F.

In a medium bowl, combine the tomatoes (and their juice), olives, onion, and garlic until mixed.

Lightly mist the fillets on both sides with olive oil and season with salt and pepper. Place in a single layer in an 11" × 7" glass or ceramic baking dish or the equivalent. Top evenly with the tomato mixture. Roast until the fish flakes easily and is no longer translucent in the center, 10 to 12 minutes.

Makes 4 servings

Per serving: 149 calories, 23 g protein, 4 g carbohydrates, 4 g fat (less than 1 g saturated), 57 mg cholesterol, trace fiber, 396 mg sodium

Biggest Loser Trainer Tip: Jillian Michaels

Want to sample a lot of these healthy recipes at one time? Have a dinner party or movie night where everyone makes and brings a healthy recipe. That way you can quickly zero in on which new, healthy recipes you really like!

TERIYAKI SALMON KEBABS

It's particularly important in this recipe to buy the thickest pieces of salmon you can find because you want hearty bites to skewer. But in general, thicker cuts are always preferable because they come from the middle of the body of the salmon. The smaller and tougher cuts come from the tail end. Since the tail does all of the "working out," it makes sense that it's leaner, and thus tougher. If you go to the fish counter and see large pieces, just ask them to cut off the top (thicker) half and buy that. More often than not, they'll happily accommodate your request.

---

1   **pound thick skinless, boneless salmon fillets, cut into 24 cubes**

24   **canned unsweetened pineapple chunks in juice, drained (about 1¼ cups)**

24   **(1") squares sweet onion**

2   **tablespoons lite or reduced-sodium teriyaki sauce**

    Olive oil spray

In a medium resealable container, combine the salmon, pineapple, and onion. Add the teriyaki sauce and gently toss. Cover and marinate in the refrigerator for 30 minutes. Soak 8 wooden skewers in water for 30 minutes (or have metal skewers ready).

Preheat a grill to high heat.

Thread 1 piece of onion, 1 piece of pineapple, and 1 piece of salmon on a skewer, then repeat 2 times on the same skewer so that all the ingredients are touching. Repeat with the remaining 7 skewers.

Lightly mist a large sheet of aluminum foil with the olive oil spray. Set the foil on the grill, oiled side up, and add the skewers. Cook 1 minute. Turn the skewers a quarter-turn. Continue cooking, turning every minute, until the fish is cooked through and pale pink in the center, 1 to 3 minutes longer. Serve immediately.

Makes 4 servings

Per serving: 271 calories, 24 g protein, 15 g carbohydrates, 13 g fat (3 g saturated), 67 mg cholesterol, 1 g fiber, 179 mg sodium

ROASTED LEMON-PEPPER SALMON

The widely available farm-raised salmon is much higher in fat than wild-caught salmon, which can be hard to find and is also usually more expensive. For this recipe I use the budget-conscious farm-raised salmon, but using wild would save you 5 grams of fat per serving. Look for wild fish on sale, in the freezer section, or if possible, at your local fresh-seafood vendor or farmers' market to save money.

Olive oil in a sprayer (not store-bought spray that contains propellant)

4 (4-ounce) skinless, boneless salmon fillets

½ teaspoon salt-free lemon-pepper seasoning

⅛ teaspoon salt, or to taste

1 lemon, cut into 4 wedges, plus more if desired

Preheat the oven to 400°F. Lightly spray an 8" × 8" glass or ceramic baking dish (or the equivalent) with olive oil.

Lightly mist both sides of each salmon fillet with olive oil and season with the seasoning and salt. Transfer the salmon to the prepared baking dish. Roast the salmon for 10 to 12 minutes, or until cooked through and pale pink in the center. Transfer to serving plates and squeeze a lemon wedge over each fillet. Serve immediately with additional lemon wedges, if desired.

Makes 4 servings

Per serving: 214 calories, 23 g protein, 1 g carbohydrates, 13 g fat (2 g saturated), 67 mg cholesterol, trace fiber, 141 mg sodium

Adam and Stacey Capers

For our family, dinnertime is an important time. It's when we reflect on our day and prepare for the next. Our daughter loves to help get dinner ready by mixing things. We explain that it's important to eat healthy, so she always wants to make sure whatever food she is eating is good for her.

MELON TZATZIKI–TOPPED SALMON

Back in my early catering days, I used to poach a whole salmon fillet, cover it in a dill sauce made with mayonnaise and sour cream, then top it with paper-thin sliced cucumbers. This dish is a much simpler, much healthier version that's equally delicious!

Basic Pan-Seared Salmon (opposite page), heated

1 cup Melon Tzatziki (page 91)

Place the warm salmon fillets on a serving platter or place one fillet on each of 4 dinner plates. Spoon ¼ cup tzatziki over each and serve.

Makes 4 servings

Per serving: 235 calories, 24 g protein, 5 g carbohydrates, 13 g fat (2 g saturated), 68 mg cholesterol, trace fiber, 190 mg sodium

BASIC PAN-SEARED SALMON

It's important to invest in an olive oil sprayer—one that you can fill with your own olive oil. The prefilled sprayers have propellant in them that shouldn't be sprayed directly on food. If the budget doesn't permit a sprayer right now, brush the fish with as little oil as possible. You need just enough to keep it moist.

4 (4-ounce) skinless, boneless salmon fillets

Olive oil in a sprayer (not store-bought spray that contains propellant)

Salt, to taste

Ground black pepper, to taste

Lightly mist the fillets all over with olive oil and season with salt and pepper.

Place a nonstick skillet large enough for the fillets to lie in a single layer over medium-high heat. When hot, add the salmon and cook until golden brown on both sides, 1 to 2 minutes per side. Reduce the heat to medium and continue to cook, turning once, until cooked through and pale pink in the center, 2 to 3 minutes per side. Serve immediately.

Makes 4 servings

Per serving: 210 calories, 23 g protein, 0 g carbohydrates, 13 g fat (2 g saturated), 67 mg cholesterol, 0 g fiber, 67 mg sodium

Coleen Skeabeck, Season 6

For me, getting the best deal possible and not breaking the bank is so important. Before I go grocery shopping I plan out what I'd like to eat for the next week or so and then buy only what I need instead of throwing a bunch of items into my cart.

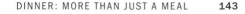

SHRIMP QUESADILLA

This quesadilla is perfect for those who enjoy mild flavors. If you have bolder tastes, feel free to add fresh cilantro or some salt-free Mexican seasoning. I call for bay shrimp to save money, but if larger shrimp are on sale, definitely swap them in . . . though you will need to cook the shrimp a bit longer and then chop them into smaller pieces.

2 teaspoons cocktail sauce

2 teaspoons fat-free sour cream

Olive oil spray

3 ounces cooked peeled bay shrimp (about ½ cup), drained

1 (7½") low-fat, low-carb, multigrain or whole wheat flour tortilla

¾ ounce finely shredded (about ⅓ cup) Cabot's 75% Light Cheddar Cheese or other low-fat Cheddar

In a small bowl, mix the cocktail sauce and sour cream until thoroughly combined.

Place a small nonstick skillet over high heat. When hot, spray with the olive oil spray. Add the shrimp and cook for 1 to 2 minutes just to remove any excess moisture and heat the shrimp through.

Place a nonstick skillet large enough for the tortilla to lie flat over medium-high heat and add the tortilla. Sprinkle about half of the cheese evenly over half of the tortilla. Top with the shrimp, followed by the remaining cheese. Fold the bare half over the filled half. Cook for about 2 minutes, or until the cheese begins to melt and the tortilla is lightly browned in spots. Carefully turn over and cook until the cheese is completely melted, 1 to 2 minutes longer.

Transfer the quesadilla to a serving plate and cut into 4 wedges. Serve immediately with the cocktail sauce mixture for dipping or dollop it on the quesadilla.

Makes 1 serving

Per serving: 285 calories, 25 g protein, 17 g carbohydrates, 5 g fat (1g saturated), 104 mg cholesterol, 8g fiber, 638mg sodium

Meat

PEPPERED POT ROAST

This roast is very low in sodium. If you're enjoying it by itself, it's best to increase the seasoned salt to ¾ teaspoon. If you're using it primarily as roast beef for sandwiches or in a salad where there is other salt, you'll need only the ¼ teaspoon listed in the ingredients.

1 teaspoon extra-virgin olive oil

1 (1¾-pound) trimmed top round roast

2 teaspoons ground black pepper

¼ teaspoon seasoned salt (I used Lawry's)

Salt, to taste

Preheat the oven to 350°F.

Rub the olive oil evenly over the roast and season with the pepper and seasoned salt. Let stand for 15 minutes.

Place a medium nonstick ovenproof skillet over medium-high heat. When hot, add the roast and sear on all sides, including the ends, until just browned, 45 to 60 seconds per side. Transfer the skillet to the oven and roast until a meat thermometer inserted in the center registers 125°F. for medium rare, 15 to 20 minutes. Loosely place a piece of foil over the roast (not the whole pan) and let stand for 10 minutes.

Slice the roast against the grain into thin slices and serve immediately, or refrigerate the whole roast then slice very thinly by hand or on a meat slicer to use as deli meat.

Makes 6 (about 4-ounce) servings

Per serving: 137 calories, 28 g protein, trace carbohydrates, 5 g fat (2 g saturated), 58 mg cholesterol, trace fiber, 123 mg sodium

CONTEMPORARY PEPPERED CHOPPED STEAK

I've been eating a version of this chopped steak practically my entire life. Real beef is used, but thanks to the lean cut, it's still significantly lightened up. I use grape juice instead of the Burgundy wine my mom often added—I love the extra sweetness that contrasts with the fresh ground black pepper coating the outside and makes it, undoubtedly, great for the whole family!

---

1 pound 96% lean ground beef

¾ cup cooked brown rice

6 tablespoons minced fresh parsley

½ teaspoon salt

4 teaspoons ground black pepper

Olive oil spray

2 cups thinly sliced sweet onion rings

1⅓ cups 100% grape juice (or one 10-ounce bottle)

¼ cup balsamic vinegar

In a large bowl, mix the beef, rice, 5 tablespoons of the parsley, and the salt until well combined. Divide the mixture into 4 equal portions and form into 1"-thick oval patties. Season evenly with the pepper, pressing it into the patties on all sides.

Place a large nonstick skillet over high heat. When hot, lightly mist with the olive oil spray. Add the patties and cook for 2 to 4 minutes per side, or until the outsides brown and the insides are very slightly less done than desired. Transfer the steaks to a platter and cover to keep warm.

Respray the pan off the heat, then place over medium heat. Add the onions and cook, stirring, for about 5 minutes, or until tender. Add the grape juice and vinegar and return the heat to high. Boil for 9 to 11 minutes, or until the liquid is reduced to about ½ cup. Place the steaks on each of 4 serving plates and top with the onions and sauce. Sprinkle with the remaining 1 tablespoon parsley and serve.

Makes 4 servings

Per serving: 271 calories, 24 g protein, 32 g carbohydrates, 5 g fat (2 g saturated), 60 mg cholesterol, 3 g fiber, 372 mg sodium

GYM RAT'S GRILLED LONDON BROIL

This steak is insanely simple. You can make it in about 15 minutes from start to finish. And it can keep you clear of roast beef from the deli counter that is often full of sodium and preservatives . . . plus deli meat is so much more expensive. If you buy London broil on sale (it's often available for $1.99/pound) you can make the whole steak for under $5. You can't even buy a pound of deli meat for that these days. Just be sure to slice it extremely thin (almost shaved) for sandwiches or cut it into small cubes (½" is great) to throw into salads. Bigger pieces and thicker slices might be tough when chilled.

½ teaspoon extra-virgin olive oil

1 (2-pound) London broil, trimmed of visible fat

1 tablespoon salt-free garlic and herb seasoning (I used Mrs. Dash)

¼ teaspoon + ⅛ teaspoon salt

Preheat a grill to high heat.

Rub the olive oil evenly over the steak and season with the seasoning and salt. Let stand 5 minutes.

Grill the steak for 5 to 6 minutes per side for medium rare, or until desired doneness. Transfer to a cutting board, cover loosely with aluminum foil, and let stand for 10 minutes.

Slice against the grain into thin slices and serve immediately, or refrigerate the whole steak, then slice very thinly by hand or on a meat slicer to use as deli meat.

Makes 6 (about 4-ounce) servings

Per serving: 150 calories, 32 g protein, 0 g carbohydrates, 5 g fat (2 g saturated), 67 mg cholesterol, 0 g fiber, 219 mg sodium

Adam and Stacey Capers, Season 6

I am amazed at the amount of grilling that we do. We grill chicken, fish, and even vegetables. We also broil and bake our food. For great flavor, we use a low-fat, low-calorie marinade or dressing.

SLOPPY JOE MEAT LOAF

Meat loaf is a great way to save money and still eat amazing food that tastes expensive. Plus, leftovers make for delicious, inexpensive, and easy sandwiches to take to work or school the next day.

Olive oil spray

⅔ cup old-fashioned oats

⅓ cup + ¼ cup + ¼ cup canned sloppy joe sauce

2 large egg whites, lightly beaten

1 pound 96% lean ground beef

⅓ cup minced green bell pepper

¼ cup finely chopped sweet onion

1 clove fresh garlic, minced

Preheat the oven 350°F. Lightly mist a 9" × 5" × 3" nonstick loaf pan (a slightly smaller one is OK) with the olive oil spray.

In a medium mixing bowl, combine the oats, ⅓ cup + ¼ cup of the sloppy joe sauce, and the egg whites. Let the mixture stand for 3 minutes, or until the oats begin to soften. Add the beef, bell pepper, onion, and garlic. With a fork or clean hands, mix the ingredients until well combined.

Transfer the mixture to the prepared pan and spread so that the top is flat. Spread the remaining ¼ cup sloppy joe sauce evenly over the top. Bake for 30 minutes, or until the meat is no longer pink in the center. Let sit for 10 minutes. Cut into 8 slices and serve.

Makes 4 servings

Per serving: 225 calories, 27 g protein, 16 g carbohydrates, 5 g fat (2 g saturated), 60 mg cholesterol, 3 g fiber, 410 mg sodium

Amanda Harmer, Season 5

Try to cook a few extra meals on the weekends or always make enough for leftovers. When you have a precooked dinner at home, you're less tempted to pull up to the drive-thru, and you won't waste your calories on food that won't keep you full and nourished.

STEAK FAJITAS

To get hot, sizzling, restaurant-style fajitas, you want to be sure to cook the steak strips in a single layer over high heat. That way, each strip of meat sears and browns on the outside, while the inside stays tender and juicy. Cooking the strips will be a very quick process (like cooking steak in a wok for a stir-fry), so make sure you watch as they cook and that you remove the meat from the pan as soon as it's done.

8 fajita-sized (about 6") low-carb, whole wheat flour tortillas

1½ teaspoons salt-free Southwest or Mexican seasoning (I used Mrs. Dash)

1 (1-pound) London broil, cut against the grain into strips

Salt, to taste

Olive oil spray

2 large green bell peppers, cut into strips

1 medium onion, cut into strips

1 tablespoon freshly minced garlic

¼ cup fat-free sour cream

½ cup fresh salsa or pico de gallo (refrigerated, not jarred), drained if watery

4 teaspoons minced seeded jalapeño chile pepper (wear plastic gloves when handling)

Preheat the oven to 400°F. Stack the tortillas on a large sheet of aluminum foil and roll the foil into a tube to enclose the tortillas. Seal the ends. Heat the tortillas in the oven for about 5 minutes, or until warm.

Sprinkle the seasoning evenly over the steak strips and season with salt. Toss the meat well.

Place a large nonstick skillet over medium-high heat. When hot, lightly mist with the olive oil spray. Add the bell peppers and cook, stirring, until beginning to soften, 3 to 5 minutes. Add the onion and garlic and cook, stirring, until tender and lightly browned, about 5 minutes. Transfer the vegetables to a bowl and cover to keep warm.

Return the skillet to high heat. When hot, respray the pan. In batches if necessary, add the steak strips in a single layer. Cook, stirring occasionally, until the meat is lightly browned on the outsides and slightly pink inside, 1 to 2 minutes. Add the sautéed vegetables and toss with the meat until warm.

Unroll the warmed tortillas. Place 2 tortillas side by side on each of 4 large dinner plates. Divide the steak mixture evenly among the tortillas and top with the sour cream and salsa or pico de gallo. Sprinkle jalapeño evenly over the fajitas and serve.

Makes 4 servings

Per serving: 322 calories, 32 g protein, 36 g carbohydrates, 8 g fat (2 g saturated), 51 mg cholesterol, 18 g fiber, 566 mg sodium

BEER-STEWED BEEF MEXICANA

Did you ever think you'd see beer in a Biggest Loser *cookbook? Well, today is your lucky day . . . especially because there's no way that your progress will be inhibited by consuming this beer-infused entrée. If sweet potatoes are too expensive, use Ore-Ida Steam n' Mash Sweet Potatoes (for more on this, see the headnote for Japanese Beef Stew on page 154).*

Please note: If you taste the meat right after it's been seared, it will be tough. Somewhere between 1½ to 2 hours into cooking it at a simmer, it will become extremely soft—the meat breaks down and becomes so tender it will literally fall apart when speared with a fork. If it's tough when you taste it, you need to cook the stew a little longer.

---

1 (1-pound) trimmed London broil or top round steak, cut into 1" cubes

1 tablespoon whole grain oat flour (white flour is OK if you're watching the budget)

⅛ teaspoon garlic powder

⅛ teaspoon salt, or to taste

Pinch of ground black pepper, or to taste

1½ teaspoons extra-virgin olive oil

1 (12-ounce) bottle beer

1 (24-ounce) container fresh pico de gallo or fresh salsa (refrigerated, not jarred)

20 ounces sweet potatoes, peeled and cut into 2" cubes

4 small zucchini, sliced into 1" rounds

In a medium bowl combine the steak, flour, garlic powder, salt, and pepper. Toss until the beef is evenly coated. Let stand for 15 minutes.

Place a large nonstick soup pot over medium-high heat. When hot, add the oil, then the beef. Cook until browned all over, about 1 minute per side. Add the beer and pico de gallo or salsa and stir to submerge the beef. Cover, reduce the heat to low, and simmer for 1 hour.

Add the sweet potatoes, making sure they are submerged in the liquid, cover, and simmer for 45 minutes longer. Gently stir in the zucchini and simmer for 10 minutes longer, or until the meat, potatoes, and vegetables are tender. Season with additional salt and pepper, if desired. Serve immediately or refrigerate in an airtight plastic container for up to 3 days.

Makes 4 servings

Per serving: 302 calories, 28 g protein, 40 g carbohydrates, 6 g fat (2g saturated), 50 mg cholesterol, 5 g fiber, 659 mg sodium

SZECHUAN BEEF AND BROCCOLI

This stir-fry cooks quickly, so be sure to have all of your ingredients prepped before you start. Watch the meat—if you overcook it or the pan isn't hot enough when you put it in, the beef could be tough.

1 (1-pound) top round steak, sliced against the grain into scant ¼"-thick strips

1 teaspoon garlic powder

Salt, to taste

Ground black pepper, to taste

Olive oil spray

1 (14-ounce) bag frozen broccoli (about 5 cups)

1 tablespoon freshly minced garlic

2 teaspoons toasted sesame oil

¼ cup bottled Szechuan stir-fry sauce

In a large bowl, combine the steak, garlic powder, salt, and pepper and toss until well combined.

Place a large nonstick skillet or nonstick wok over high heat. When hot, mist with the olive oil spray. Add the broccoli and garlic and cook, stirring, for 4 to 6 minutes, or until the garlic softens and the broccoli is heated through and crisp-tender, being careful not to burn the garlic. Transfer to a large bowl and cover to keep warm.

Return the pan to high heat and add 1 teaspoon of the sesame oil. When hot, add half of the steak in a single layer, and cook, stirring occasionally, until lightly browned on both sides, 1 to 2 minutes. Transfer the steak to the bowl with the vegetables and re-cover. Repeat with the remaining 1 teaspoon sesame oil and steak. Return all the steak and vegetables to the pan and remove from the heat. Add the sauce and mix well to coat. Divide among 4 bowls and serve.

Makes 4 servings

Per serving: 191 calories, 25 g protein, 10 g carbohydrates, 6 g fat (2 g saturated), 50 mg cholesterol, 2 g fiber, 599 mg sodium

Budget Tips from The Biggest Loser

Ask the kids to set the table with cloth napkins and real plates at family mealtime. Not only will dinner seem more special, but you won't be eating (and spending) through an ever-dwindling supply of paper and plastic.

JAPANESE BEEF STEW

If your family likes Asian flavors, this stew is likely to be a huge hit. To save prep time—and perhaps a significant amount of cash—look for Ore-Ida Steam n' Mash Sweet Potatoes in your grocer's freezer section. Sweet potatoes can be very costly at certain times of the year, so stock up on the Steam n' Mash when it's on sale. Though they are designed to be served as mashed potatoes, they come as big pieces of microwavable frozen sweet potatoes. I'm all about creative solutions: Just substitute 1 pound of the frozen sweet potatoes (no need to microwave them) in place of the fresh ones. They'll be just as nutritious . . . and definitely delicious!

Please note: If you taste the meat right after it's been seared, it will be tough. Somewhere between 1½ to 2 hours into cooking it at a simmer, it will become extremely soft—the meat breaks down and becomes so tender it will literally fall apart when speared with a fork. If it's tough when you taste it, you need to cook the stew a little longer.

---

1 tablespoon whole grain oat flour (white flour is OK if you're watching the budget)

⅛ teaspoon garlic powder

Pinch of ground black pepper, or to taste

1 (1-pound) trimmed top round steak or London broil, cut into 1" cubes

2 teaspoons toasted sesame oil

6 whole scallions, ends trimmed and chopped (about 1 cup)

1 tablespoon freshly minced garlic

In a medium bowl, combine the flour, garlic powder, and pepper. Add the steak and toss to coat. Refrigerate for at least 15 minutes.

Place a large nonstick soup pot over medium-high heat. When hot, add the oil, then the beef and cook to brown on all sides, about 1 minute per side. Reduce the heat to medium and add the scallions, garlic, and ginger. Cook, stirring occasionally with a wooden spoon and scraping any brown bits from the bottom of the pan, until the garlic is tender, about 5 minutes. Stir in the broth, soy sauce, mushrooms, and carrots, turn the heat to high, and bring to a boil. Reduce the heat to low, cover the pot, and simmer for 45 minutes (if the broth is not boiling slightly, the heat should be increased slightly).

Add the sweet potatoes, cover, and cook until the beef is tender, 45 minutes or longer. Add the snap peas and cook 5 minutes longer,

1 tablespoon minced peeled fresh ginger

2¾ cups lower-sodium, fat-free beef broth

2 tablespoons lower-sodium soy sauce

1 (6-ounce) can whole peeled straw mushrooms, drained

4 small carrots (or 2 large), peeled and cut into bite-sized rounds

1 pound sweet potatoes, peeled and cut into 1" cubes

½ pound sugar snap peas

Salt, to taste

or until the peas are tender. Season with salt and additional pepper. Serve immediately or refrigerate in an airtight plastic container for up to 3 days.

Makes 4 servings

Per serving: 291 calories, 33 g protein, 35 g carbohydrates, 6 g fat (2 g saturated), 50 mg cholesterol, 7 g fiber, 658 mg sodium

SPIRALS AND MEATBALLS

This is one of those dishes that's just as kid-friendly as spaghetti and meatballs. And you can get your kids involved in mixing and shaping the meatballs to save you time and start them feeling comfy in the kitchen at a young age. This is one time when they can play with their food!

8   ounces fiber-enriched rotini pasta (I used Ronzoni Smart Taste)

3   cups Main Event Marinara Sauce (page 162), heated

New Favorite Meatballs (page 87), heated

4   teaspoons grated reduced-fat Parmesan cheese

Cook the pasta according to package directions. Drain.

Divide the pasta among 4 serving bowls. Top each with ¾ cup sauce and 8 meatballs. Sprinkle 1 teaspoon of the Parmesan over each bowl and serve.

Makes 4 servings

Per serving: 481 calories, 37 g protein, 76 g carbohydrates, 8 g fat (2 g saturated), 63 mg cholesterol, 13 g fiber, 528 mg sodium

HOISIN-GLAZED PORK CHOPS

After much testing, I realized that it's much easier to cook pork chops perfectly when the raw chops are no thicker than ¾". If you buy pork chops that are thicker, you can pound them with a meat mallet or even simply press them out with your hand to ¾". Also, do note that broilers vary widely in heat, so the first time you make these, they may not turn out perfectly (you can always do a test-run with one chop). Ideally, the chops should be cooked to perfection when the glaze is caramelized and not burned. The timing below will be close, but might not be dead-on depending on your broiler.

Olive oil in a sprayer (not store-bought spray that contains propellant)

4 (4-ounce) trimmed, boneless pork loin chops (3½- to 4½-ounce chops are OK) about ¾" thick

1 teaspoon garlic powder

Salt, to taste

Ground black pepper, to taste

¼ cup hoisin sauce

Preheat the broiler. Line a small baking sheet with aluminum foil and lightly spray the foil with olive oil.

Lightly spray both sides of the chops with olive oil and season evenly with the garlic powder, salt, and pepper. Place the chops on the prepared baking sheet and broil about 3" from the heat for 2 minutes per side (be sure to leave the oven door open a crack when broiling). Remove from the oven and brush or spread 1½ teaspoons of hoisin over the top of each chop. Continue broiling for 1 minute longer. Turn the chops and brush each with an additional 1½ teaspoons sauce. Broil for 1 to 2 minutes longer, or until the pork is just barely pink inside and the hoisin sauce is a bit caramelized. Serve immediately.

Makes 4 servings

Per serving: 177 calories, 26 g protein, 5 g carbohydrates, 5 g fat (1 g saturated), 75 mg cholesterol, trace fiber, 261 mg sodium

HERBED PORK LOIN ROAST

When cooking pork loin, you have to be extremely careful not to overcook it or it is guaranteed to be dry. Though pork tenderloin is a bit more expensive, it's slightly leaner than pork loin and the smaller size makes it is easier to keep nice and tender. I actually love grilling tenderloins for even more flavor. If you happen to find tenderloins on sale, buy two 1-pound pork tenderloins for this recipe and grill them for about 3 minutes per side over high heat. If you're sticking with the loin, make sure you have a good meat thermometer and remember that meat continues to cook slightly once it's been removed from the oven.

1 tablespoon finely chopped fresh rosemary

1 tablespoon finely chopped fresh flat-leaf parsley

¼ teaspoon garlic powder

¼ teaspoon salt

¼ teaspoon ground black pepper

⅛ teaspoon ground red pepper

1 (2½-pound) pork loin roast, trimmed of all visible fat before weighing

2 teaspoons extra-virgin olive oil

Preheat the oven to 350°F. In a small bowl, mix the rosemary, parsley, garlic powder, salt, black pepper, and ground red pepper. Rub the roast with the olive oil, and then the herb mixture. Let stand 15 minutes.

Preheat a large nonstick ovenproof skillet to medium-high heat. Add the pork and sear on all sides (including both ends) until just browned. Transfer to the oven and roast for 30 to 35 minutes, or until a meat thermometer inserted in the center registers 158°F. Cover loosely with foil and let stand 10 minutes. Slice into thin slices, pour any pan juices over the top, and serve.

Makes 8 (4-ounce) servings

Per serving: 166 calories, 30 g protein, trace carbohydrates, 4 g fat (1 g saturated), 92 mg cholesterol, trace fiber, 148 mg sodium

Adam and Stacey Capers, Season 6

With our growing family, we decided to invest in a small freezer so we can buy meat, fish, and poultry in bulk and store until needed. It's a great cost savings.

PINEAPPLE TERIYAKI PORK CHOPS

Teriyaki chicken bowls, which have become very popular in the United States, may sound like a healthy meal... but the chicken is often cooked in a ton of oil and, more often than not, dark meat is used. My version of this popular dish uses pork, which is actually leaner than the chicken in most traditional bowls. By adding a good amount of pineapple, you'll still get that teriyaki flavor you crave, but you don't need as much sauce—a very good thing since teriyaki marinades and even reduced-sodium sauces still contain a lot of sodium. Make sure your pork chops are no thicker than ¾"—see the headnote for Hoisin-Glazed Pork Chops (page 158) for more info.

Olive oil in a sprayer (not store-bought spray that contains propellant)

4 (4-ounce) trimmed boneless pork loin chops (3½- to 4½-ounce chops are OK), about ¾" thick

1 teaspoon garlic powder

Salt, to taste

Ground black pepper, to taste

8 teaspoons honey teriyaki marinade and sauce (this is not simple teriyaki sauce— I used Ken's Steak House Marinade and Sauce)

4 slices canned pineapple slices in juice, drained

Preheat the broiler. Line a small baking sheet with aluminum foil and lightly spray the foil with olive oil.

Lightly mist both sides of the chops with olive oil and season with the garlic powder, salt, and pepper. Place the chops, not touching, on the prepared baking sheet and broil about 3" from the heat for about 2 minutes (be sure to leave the oven door open a crack when broiling). Turn the chops and brush or spread 2 teaspoons of the teriyaki marinade evenly over the top of each. Top with pineapple slices. Broil for 3 to 5 minutes longer, or until the pineapple and glaze brown lightly and the pork is barely pink inside. Serve immediately.

Makes 4 servings

Per serving: **199 calories, 26 g protein, 13 g carbohydrates, 5 g fat (1 g saturated), 75 mg cholesterol, trace fiber, 234 mg sodium**

Vegetarian

MAIN EVENT MARINARA SAUCE

Canned tomatoes will always vary slightly in taste depending on where they were packed, what time of year they were harvested, etc. So sometimes the same recipe for sauce might require a touch of salt, while another may require a hint of sweetener. Here, we added very little of each and loved the results based on our canned tomatoes. If you need to, feel free to add another hint of salt or honey. Just be sure not to overdo it.

Olive oil spray

1 cup minced yellow or white onion

2 tablespoons freshly minced garlic

1 (28-ounce) can crushed tomatoes

¼ cup water

2 tablespoons no-salt-added tomato paste

2 teaspoons honey

1 tablespoon dried oregano

2 teaspoons dried basil

½ teaspoon crushed red pepper flakes

Salt, to taste (optional)

Spray a medium nonstick saucepan with the olive oil spray and place over medium heat. Add the onion and garlic and cook until just becoming tender (they should not brown), 4 to 6 minutes. Reduce the heat to low and with a wooden spoon stir in the tomatoes, water, tomato paste, honey, oregano, basil, and pepper flakes until well combined. Cover and cook, stirring occasionally, for at least 1 hour. Season with salt, if needed.

Makes 7 (½-cup) servings; about 3½ cups sauce

Per serving: 63 calories, 3 g protein, 15 g carbohydrates, less than 1 g fat (trace saturated), 0 mg cholesterol, 3 g fiber, 156 mg sodium

Budget Tips from The Biggest Loser

Don't toss those vegetable peels! Save them to make your own stock and freeze it. It's cheaper and more flavorful than the canned stuff and can be used as a nutritious base for many soups and stews.

TOFU PARMESAN

For this recipe, you want to use light tofu, though some boxes may not actually be marked with the word "light." Just be sure to look for a brand that is 1.5 grams of fat or less per 3-ounce serving. Also, most blocks of tofu are 12 ounces, though some may range from 12.3 ounces to 12.5 ounces. Any of these options are fine for this recipe, as long as it's about 12 ounces.

2 (12-ounce) blocks extra-firm light tofu

Olive oil in a sprayer (not store-bought spray that contains propellant)

1 teaspoon garlic powder

Salt, to taste

Ground black pepper, to taste

1¾ cups Main Event Marinara Sauce (opposite page)

2½ ounces finely shredded reduced-fat mozzarella cheese (I used the Precious brand, which is Sorrento on the East Coast)

1 tablespoon grated reduced-fat Parmesan cheese

Drain the tofu well, then wrap each block separately in a few layers of paper towels or clean, lint-free dish towels. Place the wrapped tofu blocks side by side on a large dinner plate or platter. Place another plate of the same size on top of the tofu and set a heavy, large can (such as a 28-ounce canned good) or some sort of equivalent weight on top of the plate. Allow to drain for 2 hours in the refrigerator.

Preheat the oven to 400°F. Lightly mist a large nonstick baking sheet with olive oil.

Cut each drained tofu block into 8 equal slices (about ½" thick each), creating 16 slices total. Season both sides of the tofu slices evenly with the garlic powder, salt, and pepper. Set them side by side, without touching, on the prepared baking sheet. Lightly mist the tops with olive oil. Bake, gently turning once, for 20 minutes, or until the outsides begin to brown and crisp slightly.

Spread ¾ cup of the marinara sauce in an 11" × 7" glass or ceramic baking dish. Lay the baked tofu slices side by side in the dish atop the sauce. Top the tofu evenly with the remaining 1 cup sauce. Sprinkle with the mozzarella, followed by the Parmesan. Bake for 10 minutes, or until the sauce is warmed through and the cheese is melted. Serve immediately.

Makes 4 servings

Per serving: 191 calories, 19 g protein, 19 g carbohydrates, 6 g fat (less than 1 g saturated), 8 mg cholesterol, 5 g fiber, 400 mg sodium

BAKED ZITI

It may seem that baked ziti would have to be off-limits on the Biggest Loser meal plan. Fortunately, it's not so. While you don't want eat baked ziti for every meal, it's no problem to enjoy as a treat every once in awhile, thanks to reduced-fat cheese and the fiber-enriched pastas that are now available. Remember, to maintain long-term weight loss it's important not to feel deprived. Enjoying much healthier versions of your favorite "cheat foods" from time to time can help keep you on track.

Olive oil spray

1 (14½-ounce) box fiber-enriched ziti or penne rigate (I used Ronzoni Smart Taste)

1 (15-ounce) container fat-free ricotta cheese

2 large egg whites

8 ounces (4 cups) finely shredded reduced-fat mozzarella cheese

¼ teaspoon garlic powder

Salt, to taste

Ground black pepper, to taste

Crushed red pepper flakes, to taste

Main Event Marinara Sauce (page 162), or 3½ cups other low-fat, low-sodium, marinara

2 tablespoons grated reduced-fat Parmesan cheese

Preheat the oven to 450°F. Lightly mist a 13" × 9" × 2" ceramic or glass baking dish with the olive oil spray.

Cook the ziti according to package directions until al dente. Drain.

In a large mixing bowl, mix the ricotta, egg whites, and all but 1 cup of the mozzarella until well combined. Add the garlic powder and season with salt, pepper, and red pepper flakes. Stir in the cooked pasta until well combined.

Spread 1 cup of the marinara sauce on the bottom of the prepared dish. Add half of the pasta in an even layer over the sauce. Top the pasta evenly with another 1 cup sauce. Layer the remaining pasta over the sauce. Spoon the remaining 1½ cups sauce evenly over the top of the pasta, then sprinkle the remaining mozzarella and the Parmesan over the top.

Cover the dish with aluminum foil and bake for 20 minutes. Remove the foil and bake 10 minutes longer, or until the mozzarella is melted. Let stand 5 minutes. Cut into 8 pieces or spoon among 8 bowls and serve.

Makes 8 servings

Per serving: 350 calories, 22 g protein, 57 g carbohydrates, 6 g fat (3 g saturated), 20 mg cholesterol, 8 g fiber, 429 mg sodium

CHEESY BAKED SWEET POTATO

Sweet potatoes contain dietary fiber and protein and are a source of vitamins A and C, iron, and calcium. This delicious version of a classic baked potato makes a light yet satisfying vegetarian meal when paired with a side salad. If you have trouble finding a sweet potato that is exactly 6 ounces, you can follow the directions below and make two servings using two wedges of cheese and one 12-ounce potato (the larger potato will take a bit longer to cook in the microwave).

---

1 **(6-ounce) sweet potato,** scrubbed

1 wedge (¾ ounce) **Laughing Cow Light Garlic & Herb cheese**

With a fork, poke the potato 5 times on each side. Place in a microwave-safe bowl or on a microwave-safe dish. Cover the bowl or dish loosely with a paper towel and microwave on high for 5 minutes. Carefully flip the potato (it will be very hot) and microwave 3 to 5 minutes longer, or until it is tender throughout.

Cut an opening in the potato stretching 1" from each end and deep enough to open the potato completely without cutting it in half. Spread the cheese evenly in the center, mash it into the potato slightly with a fork to melt, and serve.

Makes 1 serving

Per serving: 166 calories, 5 g protein, 31 g carbohydrates, 2 g fat (1 g saturated), 10 mg cholesterol, 5 g fiber, 352 mg sodium

Sides

ROSEMARY SWEET-POTATO STEAK FRIES

I've always preferred white potatoes over sweet potatoes, so imagine my surprise when I couldn't stop eating these fries. My team and I had made them with light-skinned sweet potatoes (not the red "yams") and were shocked at how tasty they were. We pulled them out of the oven and they were practically gone in a minute. If you're a little hesitant to try sweet potatoes, but you like rosemary, this recipe may just convert you.

2	pounds sweet potatoes, peeled and cut into steak fry–sized pieces
1½	tablespoons freshly minced garlic
1½	teaspoons dried rosemary
2	teaspoons extra-virgin olive oil
¼	teaspoon salt, or to taste

Preheat the oven to 450°F.

In a large glass or plastic bowl, toss the sweet potatoes with the garlic, rosemary, olive oil, and salt. Arrange in a single layer, not touching, on a large nonstick baking sheet. Bake for 15 minutes. Turn the potato pieces and bake 10 to 15 minutes longer, or until tender inside.

Makes 6 servings

Per serving: **120** calories, **2 g** protein, **24 g** carbohydrates, **2 g** fat (trace saturated), **0 mg** cholesterol, **4 g** fiber, **169 mg** sodium

Biggest Loser Trainer Tip: Bob Harper

If you can't afford fresh vegetables all the time or don't have any handy for a recipe, stock up on frozen veggies—they're quick and easy. We keep them in *The Biggest Loser* kitchen on the ranch.

GRILLED SWEET POTATOES

Sweet potatoes vary widely in size. If you find ones that are very thick around, they may take a little longer to cook than the directions indicate below. If you do have big slices, just leave them on the grill, checking them every minute or two, until they are nice and tender in the center.

1½ pounds sweet potatoes, peeled and sliced crosswise into ¼"-thick slices

2 teaspoons extra-virgin olive oil

1 teaspoon garlic powder

1 teaspoon paprika

¼ teaspoon salt, plus more to taste

Ground black pepper, to taste

Preheat a grill to high heat.

Place the potatoes slices in a large glass or plastic mixing bowl. Drizzle with the olive oil then sprinkle with the garlic powder, paprika, salt, and pepper. Toss well to combine.

Transfer the potato slices to the grill and reduce the heat to low (or place them away from direct heat). Cook the potatoes until browned in spots and tender, 6 to 8 minutes per side. Serve immediately.

Makes 4 servings

Per serving: 159 calories, 3 g protein, 32 g carbohydrates, 2 g fat (trace saturated), 0 mg cholesterol, 5 g fiber, 231 mg sodium

Adam and Stacey Capers, Season 6

Instead of buying presliced fruits and veggies, buy produce whole and cut it up yourself. Invest in a good set of storage containers, too.

ORANGE-SPICED MASHED SWEET POTATOES

These potatoes should probably have been called Sweet Orange Sweet Potatoes . . . but that just didn't sound right. Along the lines of the popular sweet potatoes served at Thanksgiving, these are much more sweet than savory. Thus they go really well with spicy dishes.

1½ **pounds sweet potatoes, peeled and cut into ½" cubes**

½ **cup 100% orange juice (preferably freshly squeezed or "not from concentrate")**

2 **tablespoons light butter (from a tub, not stick), melted**

½ **teaspoon pumpkin pie spice, or more to taste**

Salt, to taste

Ground black pepper, to taste

Cook the sweet potatoes in large pot of boiling salted water until very tender, about 12 minutes. Drain.

In a medium glass or plastic mixing bowl, combine the potatoes, orange juice, butter, and pumpkin pie spice. With a hand mixer, beat the mixture until smooth. Season with salt and pepper and serve.

Makes 4 (about ¼-cup) servings

Per serving: 149 calories, 2 g protein, 29 g carbohydrates, 3 g fat (2 g saturated), 8 mg cholesterol, 4 g fiber, 124 mg sodium

Brady Vilcan, Season 6

I definitely would recommend involving the little ones in the preparation of a meal. I find that it makes them more open-minded to trying new things. When the plate isn't just set down in front of them and they've actually put some effort into the preparation, they're more willing to taste it!

CHIMICHURRI COUSCOUS

If you haven't heard of it, chimichurri originated in Argentina and is still quite popular there as well as in Argentinean restaurants in this country. Chimichurri is an Argentine equivalent of a pesto, but instead of basil and garlic as main ingredients it has a combination of parsley, oregano, garlic, salt, pepper, and usually another spice or two, with tons of olive oil. Though I love the flavors, I'm not a fan of all that oil (and the extra calories it imparts). Here's a great way to enjoy the true flavor of this tasty sauce without overdoing it on the oil.

1 cup whole wheat couscous

⅓ cup very finely chopped fresh parsley

¼ cup very finely chopped fresh cilantro

1 tablespoon freshly minced garlic

2 tablespoons red wine vinegar, plus more to taste

1 tablespoon extra-virgin olive oil

1 teaspoon dried oregano

⅛ teaspoon salt, plus more to taste

Ground black pepper, to taste

Cook the couscous according to package directions, omitting any butter or oil.

Add the parsley, cilantro, garlic, vinegar, olive oil, oregano, and salt to the couscous and stir well to combine. Season with additional vinegar, additional salt, and pepper and serve.

Makes 4 (1-cup) servings

Per serving: 142 calories, 4 g protein, 24 g carbohydrates, 4 g fat (less than 1 g saturated), 0 mg cholesterol, 4 g fiber, 76 mg sodium

WORCESTERSHIRE BROWN RICE

I've heard a lot of people say that they don't like brown rice . . . I used to feel the same way until I tried short-grain brown rice. It has a much nuttier flavor than long-grain brown rice. You can sometimes find short-grain in the "natural foods" section of your grocery store. If you don't see it there, try a health food store. If you buy it in bulk, it's insanely inexpensive.

2 cups cooked short-grain brown rice

½ cup finely chopped seeded tomato

1 tablespoon Worcestershire sauce

1 tablespoon finely chopped fresh parsley

⅛ teaspoon salt, or more to taste

Ground black pepper, to taste

In a medium glass or plastic mixing bowl, combine the rice, tomato, Worcestershire, parsley, and salt. Stir well to combine, season with pepper, and serve.

Makes 4 (about ½-cup) servings

Per serving: 117 calories, 3 g protein, 25 g carbohydrates, less than 1 g fat (trace saturated), trace cholesterol, 2 g fiber, 121 mg sodium

Heba Salama and Ed Brantley, Season 6

In your free time, prepare brown rice, quinoa, and whole wheat pasta—these items can be ready when you need them for a quick but balanced meal. Chef Devin advises that brown rice and pasta can last in the fridge up to 5 days, and quinoa about 2 days. And if you're making pasta, be sure to add a little sauce so it doesn't dry out.

PONZU BROWN RICE

Ponzu sauce is a citrus-based soy sauce that is most commonly served over albacore at sushi bars in this country. I happen to love it with a lot more than albacore. Look for it near the soy sauce in your grocery store.

2 cups cooked short-grain brown rice

1½ to 2 tablespoons ponzu sauce, to taste

½ teaspoon hot sesame oil

In a medium bowl, combine the rice, ponzu sauce, and sesame oil until well mixed. Serve immediately.

Makes 4 (about ½-cup) servings

Per serving: 118 calories, 2 g protein, 24 g carbohydrates, 1 g fat (trace saturated), 0 mg cholesterol, 2 g fiber, 142 mg sodium

Budget Tips from The Biggest Loser

Drink as they do at *The Biggest Loser* ranch—from refillable water bottles. Instead of tossing away plastic bottle after plastic bottle, get reusable bottles for family members to refill at home or on-the-go. It's the green, and less expensive, way to stay hydrated.

BROWN RICE WITH SCALLION CONFETTI

The same old brown rice eaten day after day can get really boring. So I'm always looking for ways to enhance it. Here crunchy bits of scallion and a small spike of hot sauce do just the trick.

2 cups cooked short-grain brown rice

¼ cup finely chopped scallions

1 teaspoon hot sauce, plus more to taste

1 teaspoon extra-virgin olive oil

⅛ teaspoon salt, or to taste

In a medium bowl, combine the rice, scallions, hot sauce, olive oil, and salt. Serve immediately.

Makes 4 (about ½-cup) servings

Per serving: 122 calories, 2 g protein, 23 g carbohydrates, 2 g fat (trace saturated), 0 mg cholesterol, 2 g fiber, 84 mg sodium

BALSAMIC-ROASTED BROCCOLI

Because broccoli has such a strong flavor, I like to add a bit of extra balsamic vinegar when I serve it with prepared balsamic vinaigrette, so there is lots of flavor without too much fat. When you're choosing a light balsamic vinaigrette, be sure to read labels: Many brands have tons of sodium and very little flavor.

Olive oil spray

5 cups broccoli florets

2 tablespoons light balsamic vinaigrette

1½ teaspoons balsamic vinegar

Preheat the oven to 400°F. Lightly mist a large nonstick baking sheet with the olive oil spray.

In a large resealable plastic bag, combine the broccoli, vinaigrette, and vinegar. Shake the bag to coat well. Arrange the broccoli in a single layer, not touching, on the prepared baking sheet. Bake for 12 to 15 minutes, or until the broccoli is crisp-tender and lightly browned. Serve immediately.

Makes 4 servings

Per serving: 38 calories, 3 g protein, 5 g carbohydrates, 1 g fat (trace saturated), 0 mg cholesterol, 3 g fiber, 142 mg sodium

Budget Tips from The Biggest Loser

When cleaning up after dinner, it's tempting to run the dishwasher each time. But if you wait until it's been completely filled with a few meals' worth of dishes, you'll save on water and energy costs.

THYME-ROASTED BUTTERNUT SQUASH

My grandmother taught me how to cook . . . then I spent years tweaking the dishes she made that origi-nally inspired my cooking talents. She used to make thyme-roasted potatoes with roasted chicken on a regular basis. Here I've taken squash and morphed it into a similar dish that your kids won't likely sus-pect to be a vegetable.

1 medium (about 3-pound) butternut squash, peeled

2 teaspoons extra-virgin olive oil

1 teaspoon dried thyme

¼ teaspoon salt, or more to taste

Ground black pepper, to taste

Preheat the oven to 400°F.

Cut the squash in half, scoop out and discard the seeds, and cut the squash into 1" cubes.

In a large glass or plastic mixing bowl, combine the squash, olive oil, thyme, salt, and pepper and toss to mix well. Transfer in a single layer, not touching, to a large nonstick baking sheet. Roast, turning the pieces once about halfway through, until tender and cooked through, about 40 minutes. Serve immediately.

Makes 4 (generous ¾-cup) servings

Per serving: 135 calories, 3 g protein, 29 g carbohydrates, 3 g fat (trace saturated), 0 mg cholesterol, 5 g fiber, 156 mg sodium

From the Experts

Out-of-season fruits and vegetables are often imported, and can be tasteless. Plan menus and choose recipes around what's currently in season. You'll enjoy better flavor *and* lower prices.

—Cheryl Forberg, RD, nutritionist for *The Biggest Loser*

EGGPLANT WITH SPICY SAUCE

Fresh ginger is quite inexpensive and a great way to add a little heat to Asian recipes and sauces. Just make sure you know how much you need before heading to the store, then break a small piece off the larger roots you'll find—it's perfectly acceptable to do that and you'll have very little waste.

---

1 teaspoon extra-virgin olive oil

1 cup chopped yellow onion

2 tablespoons minced peeled fresh ginger

2 tablespoons freshly minced garlic

1½ pounds unpeeled eggplant, cut into ¾" cubes (about 10 cups)

6 tablespoons water

¼ cup ponzu sauce

½ to 1 teaspoon chili garlic sauce, or more to taste

2 teaspoons toasted sesame oil

4 tablespoons finely chopped fresh cilantro

Place a large nonstick skillet over medium-high heat. When hot, add the olive oil, then the onion, ginger, and garlic. Cook, stirring occasionally, until the onion begins to soften, about 2 minutes. Add the eggplant and cook, stirring often, until the eggplant is lightly browned in spots and tender, 8 to 10 minutes.

Add the water, ponzu sauce, chili garlic sauce, sesame oil, and 2 tablespoons of the cilantro. Reduce the heat to medium and cover the pan. Cook, stirring occasionally, for 10 to 12 minutes, or until the eggplant is very tender and the liquid is absorbed. Transfer to a serving bowl, sprinkle with the remaining 2 tablespoons cilantro, and serve.

Makes 4 (1-cup) servings

Per serving: 107 calories, 3 g protein, 18 g carbohydrates, 4 g fat (less than 1 g saturated), 0 mg cholesterol, 7 g fiber, 447 mg sodium

SAUTÉED PEPPERED MUSHROOMS

It's very important, especially when cooking mushrooms, that you don't run them under water to wash them. Mushrooms are like sponges, so they'll soak up a lot of water, killing their flavor. Instead, dampen a paper towel and rub off any excess dirt, or peel the very thin outer layer from them. I've also found that Mrs. Dash seasonings are helpful when you're cutting down on salt.

1½ teaspoons extra-virgin olive oil

1½ pounds sliced button mushrooms

1 tablespoon freshly minced garlic

1 tablespoon Worcestershire sauce

½ teaspoon ground black pepper (freshly ground if possible)

Salt, to taste

Place a large nonstick skillet over medium-high heat. When hot, add the olive oil, then the mushrooms and garlic. Cook, stirring occasionally, until the mushrooms are tender and excess moisture is evaporated, 6 to 8 minutes. Add the Worcestershire and pepper and cook until any additional moisture is evaporated and the mushrooms are lightly browned, 7 to 9 minutes. Season with salt and serve.

Makes 4 (about ¾-cup) servings

Per serving: 61 calories, 5 g protein, 7 g carbohydrates, 2 g fat (trace saturated), trace cholesterol, 2 g fiber, 54 mg sodium

Coleen Skeabeck, Season 6

Rather than using a ton of butter to sauté veggies, I've begun using a tiny bit of olive oil and the juices of the veggies themselves. I've also found that Mrs. Dash seasonings are really helpful when you're cutting down on salt.

GREEN BEANS MARINARA

I think my dad probably ate this veggie dish more than any other as I was growing up. But when I recently served it at a taste-testing party, I was shocked: None of my friends had ever eaten this combo. It was bizarre to me since it was so common in my household. In fact, when my grandmother (the one who taught me how to cook) passed away, I went through her recipe box. She had a recipe for this dish that used a pound of green beans. At the bottom, it said, "Makes 4 servings or 1 Ben-sized serving" (that's my dad, Ben). That brought a huge smile to my face.

1   **pound green beans, trimmed**

1   **teaspoon extra-virgin olive oil**

1¼ **cups Main Event Marinara Sauce (page 162) or other low-fat, low-sodium, low-sugar marinara sauce**

Salt, to taste (optional)

Ground black pepper, to taste (optional)

Place a steamer insert in a large pot. Add enough water to reach just below the insert. Place over high heat and bring to a boil. Add the green beans to the steamer, cover, and steam for 3 to 5 minutes, or until the beans are crisp-tender. Drain and transfer to a serving bowl. Add the olive oil and toss.

Spoon the sauce over the beans, or divide the beans among 4 plates and spoon one-fourth of the sauce over each. Season with salt and pepper, if desired, and serve.

Makes 4 servings

Per serving: 77 calories, 3 g protein, 16 g carbohydrates, 2 g fat (trace saturated), 0 mg cholesterol, 6 g fiber, 97 mg sodium

GREEN PEAS WITH MINT

I use traditional peas in this recipe, not petite peas, but if the smaller peas happen to be less expensive, they are an option here. Just reduce the cooking time by about half.

Though fresh herbs are more expensive than dried ones, in some dishes they are just worth the extra money. See page 5 for suggestions on growing and freezing your own herbs.

---

2 teaspoons extra-virgin olive oil

4 cups frozen green peas

1 to 2 tablespoons finely chopped fresh mint

Salt, to taste

Ground black pepper, to taste

Place a large nonstick skillet over medium heat. Add the olive oil and then the peas and cook, stirring frequently, for 8 to 10 minutes, or until heated through. Gently stir in the mint and remove from the heat. Season with salt and pepper and serve.

Makes 4 ($^{3}/_{4}$-cup) servings

Per serving: **126 calories, 8 g protein, 18 g carbohydrates, 2 g fat (trace saturated), 0 mg cholesterol, 6 g fiber, trace sodium**

Shellay Cremen, Season 6

I used to buy all fresh veggies, but some of them ended up spoiling before I got to use them. I now use more frozen veggies. I can take out what I need and not have to worry about waste or spoilage.

COLESLAW WITH ORANGE-CILANTRO VINAIGRETTE

I've always been such a fan of coleslaw that I've made many varieties. But I really wanted to create a new, more exotic one for this book. I tried various ingredients before I struck upon the combo with orange and cilantro. I personally thought it could use even a bit more cilantro, but my test kitchen team overruled me, saying that the ⅓ cup is the perfect amount. If you're like me, feel free to add a touch more. Either way, it's a great, refreshing way to enjoy coleslaw with a fraction of the fat and calories of traditional versions.

¼ cup fat-free plain yogurt

¼ cup light mayonnaise

¼ cup 100% orange juice (preferably freshly squeezed or "not from concentrate")

3 tablespoons white vinegar

1½ teaspoons honey

7 cups shredded green cabbage (about 10 ounces)

1 cup shredded carrots

½ cup slivered red onion

⅓ cup fresh cilantro, chopped

Salt, to taste

Ground black pepper, to taste

In a large, resealable plastic container, whisk together the yogurt, mayonnaise, juice, vinegar, and honey. Add the cabbage, carrots, onion, and cilantro and stir until well combined. Season with salt and pepper. Cover and refrigerate for at least 3 hours or up to 2 days.

Makes 6 (generous ¾-cup) servings

Per serving: 83 calories, 2 g protein, 13 g carbohydrates, 3 g fat (trace saturated), 3 mg cholesterol, 3 g fiber, 118 mg sodium

CUCUMBER WEDGES

This dish is a fun, much less fattening take on the popular steakhouse Blue Cheese Iceberg Wedge. It's simple; it's quick; and it allows me (and you!) to eat tomatoes and ranch dressing, two of my favorites—what's not to love?

2 medium cucumbers

1 cup chopped tomatoes

3 tablespoons finely chopped red onion

¼ cup low-fat ranch dressing (I used the Follow Your Heart brand)

   Salt, to taste

   Ground black pepper, to taste

Place a fork at one end of one of the cucumbers and scrape along the length (almost as if you are raking dirt), creating a pattern alternating peel, no peel. Repeat around the entire cucumber, then repeat with the second cucumber. (This will break down the peel, making the cucumbers more tender). Trim the ends and cut each cucumber in half lengthwise. Remove and discard the seeds, then cut each half crosswise in half.

Arrange all 8 wedges, side by side and cut side up, on a serving platter (or place 2 on each of 4 appetizer plates). Top evenly with the tomatoes, followed by the onion. Decoratively drizzle dressing over each cucumber wedge, dripping some on the surrounding area on the plate. Season with salt and pepper and serve.

Makes 4 servings

Per serving: 38 calories, 2 g protein, 5 g carbohydrates, less than 1 g fat (trace saturated), 0 mg cholesterol, 2 g fiber, 83 mg sodium

CONTEMPORARY CAPRESE SALAD

If you long for Caprese salad (it's that salad generally found in Italian restaurants with sliced tomatoes, big hunks of fresh buffalo mozzarella and fresh basil drizzled—or should I say, doused—with olive oil) as much as I do, this recipe is definitely one to try. Now I'm not going to pretend that it tastes like the traditional version—it couldn't possibly. However, it's pretty, it's simple, and it's been satisfying my cravings for years. I'm guessing it's likely to become a staple in your house, too . . . especially if you make it in the summer when tomatoes are at their delicious peak.

4 medium tomatoes, cut into ¼"-thick slices

Olive oil in a sprayer (not store-bought spray that contains propellant)

Salt, to taste

Ground black pepper, to taste

2 ounces (1 cup) finely shredded low-fat mozzarella cheese

¼ cup finely slivered fresh basil

Place one tomato slice in the center of a large plate or round platter. Arrange the remaining slices, overlapping slightly, to form rings around the first slice. Lightly mist the tomatoes with olive oil and season with salt and pepper. Starting in the center, sprinkle the cheese evenly over the tomatoes, covering all but about ½" of the outer edge (as if you were sprinkling cheese on a pizza). Sprinkle the basil evenly over the cheese and serve.

Makes 4 servings

Per serving: 64 calories, 5 g protein, 8 g carbohydrates, 2 g fat (less than 1 g saturated), 5 mg cholesterol, 1 g fiber, 105 mg sodium

7

Dessert: Yes, There's Room for It

Even on the Biggest Loser ranch, there's a day each week when the rules are relaxed a bit and the contestants are allowed a splurge. But the operative word here is *day*—not *week* or *month* or even *year*. What Biggest Losers leave behind is dessert as an everyday thing, not dessert altogether. Long-term healthy eating requires a treat every now and again to make it a sustainable lifestyle.

When planning for a sweet, take advantage of fresh ingredients mixed with convenient low-fat, sugar-free options. This is a much better way to go than grabbing one of those highly processed, prepackaged desserts, which are not such a good deal nutritionally or calorically (not to mention economically, with all the extra packaging), points out Greg Hottinger, RD, a nutrition expert on BiggestLoserClub.com message boards.

"These overly processed snacks contain too much sugar (some have more than 2 teaspoons of sugar per pack); are sweetened with high-fructose corn syrup, which may increase obesity risk; contain little or no fiber; and are made with white flour and hydrogenated oils, which contribute to heart disease and diabetes," says Hottinger. "Even though these easy desserts may satisfy your brain's desire to eat, it does little to nourish your body. While these foods have a good shelf life, they aren't good for *your* shelf life."

The show's blue-team trainer, Bob Harper, is the first to admit that the last thing he would tell one of his contestants is "You'll never eat chocolate again." Such statements make the forbidden dessert that much more mysterious and give chocolate a lot of power over your thoughts and food daydreams. In fact, having a 1-ounce nibble of dark chocolate every now and then can be good for you! Studies have shown that dark chocolate contains antioxidants that fight high blood pressure and heart disease.

And we all know that in a house full of kids, making sweets a no-no is going to achieve exactly the opposite effect. So train your family to expect the occasional treat, not one every day.

Cheryl Forberg, RD, nutritionist for the show, says her favorite dessert is fruit. "It's amazing how quickly a few berries or a slice of melon can satisfy a craving for something sweet." You'll see how Chef Devin Alexander takes fruit up a notch, when the occasion demands, with Creamy Cherry Sorbet, Bananas with Caramel, or Strawberries with Hot Fudge. And if convincing your kids to eat fruit is a challenge, maybe pairing it with a little chocolate every now and again wouldn't be a bad tactic. Sweet!

CHOCOLATE-ORANGE PIE-LETS

If you like the bitterness of orange marmalade, you'll love the taste of these no-bake miniature pies. They definitely have that burst of bitter orange that I love. If you're not the biggest fan, simply substitute straw-berry or raspberry preserves.

Note that it's easy to crush the cereal with a mini food processor, or you can simply place in a reseal-able plastic bag and pound the bag with the flat side of a meat mallet until you have crumbs—it's a great task for the kids.

½ cup crunchy high-fiber, low-sugar cereal (such as Grape-Nuts), finely crushed into crumbs

2 tablespoons + 2 teaspoons 100% fruit orange marma-lade

1¾ cups fat-free milk

1 (1.4-ounce) package sugar-free, fat-free chocolate pudding mix

In a small mixing bowl, combine the cereal crumbs and 2 tablespoons of the marmalade and stir to mix well. Divide the mixture among 4 ramekins or small dessert bowls and press into the bottoms.

In a medium mixing bowl, combine the milk and pudding mix and whisk to blend. Pour into the ramekins or bowls. Dollop ½ teaspoon marmalade on top of each. Cover with plastic wrap and refrigerate for at least 1 hour or up to 3 days.

Makes 4 servings

Per serving: 152 calories, 7 g protein, 32 g carbohydrates, less than 1 g fat (trace saturated), 2 mg cholesterol, 3 g fiber, 407 mg sodium

Lisa Andreone, Season 1

Midnight snacks don't have to be your downfall—just make them healthy.

CHOCOLATE CHERRY TRUFFLES

When I do cooking demos around the country, I always start with, "There are two things you need to know about me: One: I lost 55 pounds and have kept it off for over 15 years; and two: I eat chocolate every day." Recipes like this one help me eat chocolate without consequence.

¼ cup dried cherries

¼ cup + 2 tablespoons old-fashioned oats

1½ tablespoons sugar-free, fat-free hot fudge

1 tablespoon + 2 teaspoons unsweetened cocoa powder

Place the cherries in the bowl of a mini food processor fitted with a chopping blade. Process until very finely chopped and sticking together. With a spatula, transfer the cherries to a medium mixing bowl. Add the oats, hot fudge, and 1 tablespoon of the cocoa powder. Using your hands or an electric mixer fitted with beaters, mix well.

Spoon the remaining 2 teaspoons cocoa powder into a small shallow bowl.

Working quickly so the fudge does not melt, divide the mixture into six equal parts (about 1 tablespoon each). Carefully form each into a ball.

Roll each ball in the cocoa powder until evenly coated. When all of the balls have been coated with the cocoa, place in a sieve and carefully bump the side of the sieve with the palm of your hand repeatedly to shake off excess cocoa powder (if there is too much cocoa on the outsides, the first bite will be bitter). Serve immediately or refrigerate in a resealable plastic container lined with waxed paper for up to 1 week.

Makes 6 truffles

Per serving: 56 calories, 2 g protein, 11 g carbohydrates, trace fat (0 g saturated), 0 mg cholesterol, 1 g fiber, 6 mg sodium

CHOCOLATE TOFFEE "SUNDAE"

This recipe should probably be called the Kimmi Dove Signature Sundae. I was hanging out with Kimmi recently, who you likely remember from the Engaged Couples edition of The Biggest Loser, *and she was telling me about this "sundae" that she and her friends have loved for years. I was a little doubtful as she described it, but with one bite, my whole kitchen team and I understood why Kimmi was raving about it. The best part is that you can customize this dessert by using any flavor combination of rice cake and pudding cup. You can try a different sundae each time you make it!*

---

1 (106-gram) double-chocolate sugar-free, fat-free pudding snack cup

1 (15-gram) Quaker Cracker Jack Butter Toffee rice cakes

2 tablespoons frozen fat-free whipped topping, thawed

Spoon about one-third of the pudding into a parfait glass or sundae dish. Crumble the rice cake on top. Top with the remaining pudding, followed by the whipped topping and serve.

Makes 1 serving

Per serving: 135 calories, 3 g protein, 30 g carbohydrates, 2 g fat (1 g saturated), 0 mg cholesterol, 1 g fiber, 245 mg sodium

WATERMELON SLUSHIES

Sometimes a piece of fruit is what you should be eating, but the same old fruit doesn't always satisfy. Well, here's a new twist on good old-fashioned watermelon that's exceptionally refreshing poolside—or anywhere else during the summer!

4 cups 1" cubes seedless watermelon, frozen

Place the frozen watermelon in a medium glass or plastic mixing bowl. Using a potato masher, mash the watermelon until it becomes slushy in texture. Divide among 4 dessert bowls and serve immediately.

Makes 4 (about $1/3$-cup) servings

Per serving: 46 calories, less than 1 g protein, 11 g carbohydrates, trace fat (trace saturated), 0 mg cholesterol, less than 1 g fiber, 2 mg sodium

DRUNKEN APPLES

I've always loved the way apples taste in fruit salad after they've been soaking in fruit juice for a day. This recipe is an easy way to recreate that flavor without having to invest in so many varieties of fruit.

1 medium apple (any variety), cored and chopped

½ cup 100% orange juice (preferably freshly squeezed or "not from concentrate")

Place the apple in a medium resealable plastic container and pour the orange juice over so all the pieces are covered. Refrigerate at least a couple hours before serving, or up to 1 day.

Makes 1 serving

Per serving: 152 calories, trace protein, 39 g carbohydrates, trace fat (trace saturated), 0 mg cholesterol, 4 g fiber, 15 mg sodium

Budget Tips from The Biggest Loser

When buying fruit like apples and oranges, it's much more cost-effective to purchase a large bag instead of weighing out a few items individually and paying per pound. If you end up with a lot of extra fruit, you can always use it to make a big, delicious fruit salad for the whole family.

GRAPE "GRANITA"

Lots of folks enjoy frozen grapes, but I've never been one for biting into anything that cold. This variation of that icy treat is a simple and fun solution that allows my teeth to take a little rest. Though it is not a true granita, it satisfies like one.

Note that this recipe makes only two servings—that's because it needs to be made and eaten immediately. If the whole family is enjoying it together, simply use 4 cups grapes and 4 teaspoons honey.

---

2 cups seedless grapes, frozen (red and black grapes make this pretty)

2 teaspoons honey

Place the grapes and honey in a food processor fitted with a chopping blade. Process, scraping down the bowl of the processor if necessary, until the grapes are very finely chopped and mostly smooth in texture. Divide between 2 chilled martini glasses or dessert bowls and serve.

Makes 2 (generous ¾-cup) servings

Per serving: 135 calories, 1 g protein, 27 g carbohydrates, less than 1 g fat (trace saturated), 0 mg cholesterol, 2 g fiber, 3 mg sodium

Biggest Loser Online Club: Juliana O'Hare, Season 6

Once a week, I head to a store with great fresh produce. I buy a variety of vegetables and fruit. When I get home, I immediately wash and cut up all the produce. I divide up the fruit and veggies and store them in one large Tupperware container and five small snack containers or Ziploc steam bags for dinner each day. Any fruit left over at the end of the week goes into my freezer to use for delicious fruit smoothies worthy of dessert status.

Change your life today! Log on to www.biggestloserclub.com and get started

BANANAS WITH CARAMEL

It seems that many people are huge fans of caramel. Too often caramel contains tons of butter, but fortunately there are alternatives. This dish allows you to enjoy the caramel flavor you love without the sugar and fat. Plus, you get much-needed potassium from the bananas. To make this for the whole family at once, use 4 small bananas and 4 tablespoons caramel sauce.

1 small (6") banana, sliced into ½" rounds

1 tablespoon jarred sugar-free caramel sauce

Place the banana in a small bowl. Heat the caramel sauce in a small bowl in the microwave or in the top of a double boiler set over simmering water until warmed, 10 to 30 seconds. Drizzle the caramel sauce over the banana and serve.

Makes 1 serving

Per serving: 135 calories, 1 g protein, 35 g carbohydrates, trace fat (trace saturated), 0 mg cholesterol, 3 g fiber, 31 mg sodium

STRAWBERRY WAFFLECAKES

Sure, you're familiar with strawberry shortcake . . . it's just about the perfect summer treat. Well, here's a new warm-weather fave that's likely to please a crowd of any size and any age—and it certainly doesn't hurt that you don't have to slave over it for more than a couple of minutes.

4 low-fat, whole grain or whole wheat waffles

2 cups sliced fresh strawberries

½ cup fat-free frozen whipped topping, thawed

Toast the waffles according to package directions. Place one waffle on each of 4 plates and mound ½ cup strawberries on top. Spoon 2 tablespoons whipped topping over each and serve.

Makes 4 servings

Per serving: 113 calories, 3 g protein, 23 g carbohydrates, 1 g fat (trace saturated), 0 mg cholesterol, 3 g fiber, 221 mg sodium

CREAMY CHERRY SORBET

It's not hard to find fat-free sorbet at the grocery store . . . but it will probably contain a ton of sugar. This creamy, delicious sorbet is chock-full of cherries but not full of sugar. If the cherries were picked at the peak of season, they'll be sweet enough without any sweetener. If they aren't peak-season and are at all bitter, a couple packets of sugar substitute will do the trick.

3 cups frozen cherries

⅔ cup fat-free, sugar-free vanilla yogurt

2 teaspoons lime juice, preferably freshly squeezed

2 to 4 (.035-ounce) packets sugar substitute (such as Splenda), to taste (optional)

Place the cherries in a food processor fitted with a chopping blade and process until just finely chopped. Quickly add the yogurt and lime juice and process just until well combined. Stir in the sugar substitute, if using. Divide among 4 martini glasses or bowls and serve.

Makes 4 (about ⅔-cup) servings

Per serving: 88 calories, 3 g protein, 20 g carbohydrates, trace fat (0 g saturated), less than 1 g cholesterol, 2 g fiber, 22 mg sodium

STRAWBERRY-LIMEADE SMOOTHIE

I've always been a big fan of strawberry lemonade and I love limeade. Here I've combined these two flavors to create a strawberry-limeade smoothie. I use Fiber One's key lime pie–flavored yogurt to add extra fiber—it'll fill you up. If you can't find it, or if it's not in your budget, you can use any lime yogurt. You won't get as much fiber, but it will still be delicious!

1½ cups frozen strawberries

6 ounces fat-free, fiber-enriched key lime pie–flavored yogurt

¼ cup fat-free milk

Zest of 1 lime (about 1½ teaspoons)

2 tablespoons freshly squeezed lime juice

Sugar substitute (such as Splenda), to taste (optional)

In a blender with ice crushing ability, combine the strawberries, yogurt, milk, lime zest and juice, and sugar substitute, if using. Blend on high speed or Ice Crush setting until smooth.

Makes 1 serving

Per serving: **228** calories, **9 g** protein, **55 g** carbohydrates, **trace fat** (trace saturated), **8 mg** cholesterol, **13 g** fiber, **134 mg** sodium

From the Experts

Your health today and tomorrow depends on the quality of foods that you choose to eat consistently. The costs incurred later in life are not just financial. Costs are measured in terms of suffering, pain, and loss of functioning. Many people maintain excellent health, save thousands of dollars each year, and avoid the need for costly medications just by choosing a healthy diet.

—Greg Hottinger, RD, nutrition expert for BiggestLoserClub.com

ORANGE CREAM SMOOTHIE

Every time I've worked on a show or book involving kids, the nutritionist always encourages me to use as much yogurt and milk in my recipes as possible—it's so important for the kids' growing bones. Yogurt used to be a tough sell for kids. But now with all of the creative flavors, from Boston cream pie to pineapple upside-down cake to key lime pie (many of which even have added fiber for extra health benefits), it's easy to create delicious dishes that employ yogurt.

1 cup frozen mango cubes

½ cup fat-free, sugar-free orange yogurt

2 tablespoons 100% orange juice (preferably freshly squeezed or "not from concentrate")

¼ teaspoon vanilla extract

4 ice cubes

In a blender with ice-crushing ability, combine the mango, yogurt, orange juice, vanilla, and ice. Make sure the lid is on tight. Using the Puree or Ice Crush setting, blend until relatively smooth. Then blend on the Liquefy setting or high speed until completely smooth. Transfer to a glass and serve.

Makes 1 smoothie

Per serving: 212 calories, 6 g protein, 49 g carbohydrates, trace fat (trace saturated), 3 mg cholesterol, 4 g fiber, 82 mg sodium

Biggest Loser Trainer Tip: Jillian Michaels

As you start stocking up your kitchen, do a junk food sweep. Get rid of anything that might trigger an overeating episode. If the junk food's not around, you won't eat it.

CULTURED PURPLE COW

Instead of using ice cream, join me for a healthy twist on this old-fashioned favorite and freeze a container of fiber-enriched vanilla yogurt. If you're serving the whole family at once, fill 4 glasses each with 1 cup of juice and ½ cup of yogurt.

---

1 cup light grape juice, chilled

1 (4-ounce) container fat-free, fiber-enriched vanilla yogurt, frozen

Pour the juice into a 16-ounce glass. Add the yogurt and stir well until it is incorporated. Serve immediately with a straw, if desired.

Makes 1 serving

Per serving: 150 calories, 4 g protein, 37 g carbohydrates, 0 g fat, 5 mg cholesterol, 5 g fiber, 145 mg sodium

STRAWBERRIES WITH HOT FUDGE

This recipe is really easy to make for the whole family (or just for yourself) and it is sure to stave off any chocolate cravings morning, noon, or night.

---

1 tablespoon sugar-free, fat-free hot fudge

1 cup quartered fresh strawberries, stems removed

Heat the hot fudge in the microwave or in the top of double boiler over simmering water until melted, about 20 seconds. Place the strawberries in a small deep bowl, drizzle the fudge on top, and serve.

Makes 1 serving

Per serving: 96 calories, 1 g protein, 23 g carbohydrates, trace fat (trace saturated), 0 mg cholesterol, 3 g fiber, 69 mg sodium

Jerry Skeabeck, Season 6

Food is definitely fuel for the body. The right type of fuel must go into it to make it work efficiently. Preplan your day's calories. In this fast-paced world, days will come when you must make quick decisions on what to eat. Remember your goal and choose wisely.

PEANUT BUTTER–TOPPED WAFFLES

This recipe is great served as a dessert, but also makes for a quick, out-the-door breakfast option—especially for the kids. It has the same appeal as some of the sugary toaster treats, but is made with much more wholesome ingredients.

4   low-fat, whole grain or whole wheat waffles

2   tablespoons reduced-fat peanut butter

Toast the waffles according to package directions. Place a waffle on each of 4 plates and spread ½ tablespoon of peanut butter evenly over each. Serve immediately.

Makes 4 servings

Per serving: 119 calories, 4 g protein, 18 g carbohydrates, 4 g fat (less than 1 g saturated), 0 mg cholesterol, 2 g fiber, 277 mg sodium

PEANUT BUTTER–FUDGE SUNDAE

There was a time when eating fat-free ice cream made no sense because it just wasn't very good. But these days, especially since the churning technology has taken over the market, healthier ice cream can actually taste very rich and creamy. If you haven't tried fat-free ice cream in a while, keep an open mind. It really can be quite tasty—with one bite, you'll definitely be glad you didn't eat the full-fat stuff!

2 teaspoons chocolate syrup

1½ teaspoons reduced-fat peanut butter

½ cup fat-free churned chocolate cookies and cream (chocolate or vanilla are good too) ice cream (I used Breyers)

1 tablespoon fat-free aerosol whipped topping

In a small bowl, stir together the syrup and peanut butter until well combined.

Spoon the ice cream into a small dessert bowl. Drizzle the peanut butter mixture over the ice cream, top with the whipped topping, and serve.

Makes 1 serving

Per serving: 195 calories, 5 g protein, 37 g carbohydrates, 3 g fat (less than 1 g saturated), trace cholesterol, 4 g fiber, 143 mg sodium

CHOCOLATE–PEANUT BUTTER GRAHAMWICHES

In my view, the only thing better than chocolate, is chocolate AND peanut butter. This harmless combo is a great occasional treat. Sure it's not a bowl of fresh berries, but there's something to be said for necessary indulgence in moderation.

4   whole chocolate graham cracker sheets

4   teaspoons reduced-fat peanut butter

½   cup frozen fat-free whipped topping, thawed

Break each graham cracker in half (so each half is 1 square). Spread 1 teaspoon peanut butter evenly over the inside of each of 4 halves. Spread 2 tablespoons whipped topping each evenly among the insides of the 4 remaining halves. Sandwich the crackers together to form 4 sandwiches, each with a layer of peanut butter and a layer of whipped topping. Transfer to an airtight plastic container and place in the freezer. Freeze for about 2 hours or up to 1 month. Serve frozen.

Makes 4 servings

Per serving: 112 calories, 2 g protein, 18 g carbohydrates, 4 g fat (less than 1 g saturated), 0 mg cholesterol, less than 1 g fiber, 142 mg sodium

References

"The Importance of Family Dinners." The National Center on Addiction and Substance Abuse (CASA), Columbia University (September 2005). www.casacolumbia.org/absolutenm/articlefiles/ 380-Importance%20of%20Family%20Dinners%20IV.pdf

Fisher, Jennifer Orlet, et al. "Parental Influence on Eating Behavior: Conception to Adolescence." *The Journal of Law, Medicine & Ethics* 35, no. 1 (Spring 2007): 22.

Florence, Michelle D., et al. "Diet quality and academic performance." *Journal of School Health* 78, no. 4 (April 1, 2008): 209(7).

Fulkerson, Jayne A., et al. "Family Meals: Perceptions of Benefits and Challenges among Parents of 8- to 10-Year-Old Children." American Dietetic Association. *Journal of the American Dietetic Association* 108, no. 4 (April 2008): 706.

Gillman, Matthew W., et al. "Family Dinner and Diet Quality Among Older Children and Adolescents." *Archives of Family Medicine* 9, no. 3 (2000): 235–240.

Gross, Kate. "Family meals help overweight teens." *Youth Studies Australia* 26, no. 4 (December 2007): 7(1).

Larson, Nicole I., et al. "Family Meals during Adolescence Are Associated with Higher Diet Quality and Healthful Meal Patterns during Young Adulthood." American Dietetic Association. *Journal of the American Dietetic Association* 107, no. 9 (October 2007): 1502.

Mahoney, Caroline R., et al. "Effect of breakfast composition on cognitive processes in elementary school children." *Elsevier, Physiology & Behavior* 85 (2005): 635–645.

Olshansky, S. J., et al. "A Potential Decline in Life Expectancy in the United States in the 21st Century," *New England Journal of Medicine* 352, no. 11 (March 17, 2005): 1138–1145.

Rockett, Helaine R. H. "Family Dinner: More Than Just a Meal." American Dietetic Association. *Journal of the American Dietetic Association* 107, no. 9 (September 2007): 1498.

Resources

Want to know what's in season in your region? Check out some of these sites:

What's Fresh Near You

www.nrdc.org/health/foodmiles/

Seasonal Fruits and Vegetables by Region

http://localfoods.about.com/od/searchbyregion/Search_Seasonal_Fruits_Vegetables_By_Region.htm

Pick Your Own

www.pickyourown.org/

Field to Plate

www.fieldtoplate.com/guide.php

For more detailed information about what food costs around the country, take a look at these Web sites:

Consumer Price Index News Releases Issued by BLS Regional Information Offices

www.bls.gov/cpi/cpi_regreleases.htm

How Much Do Americans Pay for Fruits and Vegetables?

www.ers.usda.gov/Data/FruitVegetableCosts/

Food CPI, Prices, and Expenditures: Analysis and Forecasts of the CPI for Food

www.ers.usda.gov/Briefing/cpifoodandexpenditures/consumerpriceindex.htm

Center for Science in the Public Interest, a leading health watchdog

www.cspinet.org/

Contributors

Devin Alexander, *New York Times* best-selling author and professional chef, is the host of *Healthy Decadence with Devin Alexander* on FitTv and has shared her secrets for unbelievably decadent, yet healthy foods through frequent appearances on the *Today* show, *Good Morning America, The View, The Biggest Loser,* Discovery Health's National Body Challenge, FOX, HGTV, USA, Style Network, and others and through more than 200 features in national magazines including *Prevention, Women's Health, Men's Health, Shape,* and *Healthy Cooking.* Devin has also served as culinary advisor to *Men's Fitness* magazine and cooking expert for *Women's Health* magazine.

Devin is the author of *Fast Food Fix, The Biggest Loser Cookbook,* and *The Most Decadent Diet Ever!* She speaks (and cooks) regularly throughout the country and loves receiving recipe suggestions from friends and fans at her Web site: www.devinalexander.com.

Melissa Roberson is the editor of BiggestLoserClub.com, the Web site that offers food, fitness, and exercise tips. She often visits the ranch and interviews trainers and contestants about their inspiring weight-loss journeys. She is a Web veteran, having worked on new media projects for Time Inc., the *New York Times,* News Corps., Amazon.com, and BarnesandNoble.com. She lives in Hoboken, New Jersey.

Acknowledgments

can't even express how lucky I feel to be back in Biggest Loser camp. And it's all because of so many amazing folks who've lent so much support:

Thanks to Julie Will, who worked with me day in and day out, proving to be nothing shy of awesome. To Chad Bennett, who is simply in a league of his own.

To the team at Rodale, most notably Robin Shallow and Steve Murphy, who have continually supported me. Thanks also to Christina Gaugler, Nancy N. Bailey, Wendy Hess Gable, Mitch Mandel, Diane Vezza, and Pam Simpson.

To the producers and executives of *The Biggest Loser*, particularly Mark Koops, Managing Director at Reveille; Cindy Chang at NBC Universal; and Todd Nelson and J. D. Roth, of 3 Ball Productions, who made me the happiest girl ever when they invited me into the Biggest Loser family the first time around. To Kim Niemi and Neysa Gordon, from NBC Universal, and to Dave Broome and Yong Yam, from 25/7 Productions, all of whom were integral throughout the process.

To the Biggest Loser casts, who've shared their cravings and frustrations in healthy eating that constantly inspire so many of my creations.

To Jillian Michaels and Bob Harper, for embracing me and my work. And to Melissa Roberson, who worked diligently on the nonrecipe aspects of the book, and whom I've just adored since the day I met her.

To the ever professional and fun Erin Sayers, Alexandra Gudmundsson, Emily Adams, and Sandy Levin, who methodically tested each recipe. And to Stephanie Farrell, Erin Sayers, and Kathryn Jacoby, who were integral in developing numerous dishes. To Sarah Tricomi, who supported our every move in and out of the kitchen. And to Bob Alder, for lending support and sharing some of Roman's faves.

To the team at Circulon, for continually providing me the best nonstick cookware on the market.

And a very special thanks to my manager, Julie Carson May; my publicists, Carrie Simons and Mary Lengle; and my office manager, Stephanie Farrell, all of whom not only make my career doable but provide so much love and support, as only true friends can do!

Index

Underscored page references indicate boxed text. **Boldfaced** page references indicate photographs.

P

Parmesan cheese
Grilled Chicken Parmesan, **116**, 117
Meatball Lovers' Must-Have Family-Sized Meatball Parmesan Sub, 54, **55**
Tofu Parmesan, 163

Pasta (whole grain)
Baked Ziti, 164, **165**
best choices, 11
Chimichurri Couscous, 170
preparing ahead, 171
Spirals and Meatballs, **156**, 157

Peaches
Strawberry-Peach Paradise Smoothie, 38

Peanut butter
Chocolate–Peanut Butter Grahamwiches, 210, **211**
Crunchy Bugs on a Log, 102
Peanut Butter–Fudge Sundae, **208**, 209
Peanut Butter–Topped Waffles, 207

Peas
Green Peas with Mint, 180
Japanese Beef Stew, 154–55, **155**

Peppers. *See* Bell peppers; Chile peppers

Pickles, eating in moderation, 12

Pies
Chocolate-Orange Pie-Lets, 189

Pineapple
Cherry-Pineapple Smoothie, 39, **39**
Pineapple Teriyaki Pork Chops, 160, **161**
Teriyaki Salmon Kebabs, 140
Thin and Crispy Gourmet Hula Pizza, **84**, 85

Pizza
Thin and Crispy Gourmet Hula Pizza, 84, 85

Popcorn
Trail Corn, **104**, 105

Pork
ground, buying, xv
Ham and Asparagus Omelet, 32, 33
Herbed Pork Loin Roast, 159
Hoisin-Glazed Pork Chops, 158
Pineapple Teriyaki Pork Chops, 160, **161**
Pork Sandwich, 61
slicing against the grain, xvi
"Stuffed Cabbage" Strata, 134–35, **135**
Wild West Frittata, 18, **19**

Potatoes. *See* Sweet potatoes

Poultry. *See also* Chicken; Turkey
buying and freezing, 121

Protein
animal, sources of, 10
best choices, 10–11
daily servings, 10–11
low-fat dairy, sources of, 11
serving sizes, 10–11
vegetarian, sources of, 11

Q

Quesadillas
Shrimp Quesadilla, 144

Quinoa, preparing ahead, 171

R

Raisins
Crunchy Bugs on a Log, 102

Recipes, technique notes for, xvi–xvii

Rice
Bench Press Bell Peppers, 131
brown, short grain, buying, xiv
Brown Rice with Scallion Confetti, 173
Contemporary Peppered Chopped Steak, 146, **147**
Ponzu Brown Rice, 172
preparing ahead, 171
"Stuffed Cabbage" Strata, 134–35, **135**
Worcestershire Brown Rice, 171

Ricotta cheese
Baked Ziti, 164, **165**

S

Salads and dressings
Berry–Mixed Green Salad with Grilled Chicken, **72**, 73
Coleslaw with Orange-Cilantro Vinaigrette, 181
Contemporary Caprese Salad, **184**, 185
Greek Salad with Grilled Chicken, 76–77
Greek Vinaigrette, 77
Salmon Spinach Salad, 71
Spinach Salad with Feta and Mandarin Oranges, 74, **75**

Salmon
Basic Pan-Seared Salmon, 143
Melon Tzatziki–Topped Salmon, 142, **142**
Roasted Lemon-Pepper Salmon, 141
Salmon Burgers, 47
Salmon Spinach Salad, 71
Teriyaki Salmon Kebabs, 140

Salsa
Kiwi-Watermelon Salsa, 98, **99**

Sandwiches. *See also* Burgers
Bacon, Egg, and Cheese Breakfast Sandwich, 28, **29**
BBQ-Bacon Meat Loaf Sandwich, 62
Chicken Salad Dijon with Grapes and Apple, **66**, 67
Family-Sized Chicken Cheese Steak, 132
Family-Sized Roast Beef Sub, 60
Meatball Lovers' Must-Have Family-Sized Meatball Parmesan Sub, 54, **55**
Mediterranean Chicken Sandwich, 64, **65**
Open-Faced Roast Beef Sandwich, 81
Ranch Burger Pocket, 53
Spinach, Egg, and Cheese Breakfast Wrap, 30, 31

Also available in the *New York Times* best-selling Biggest Loser series...

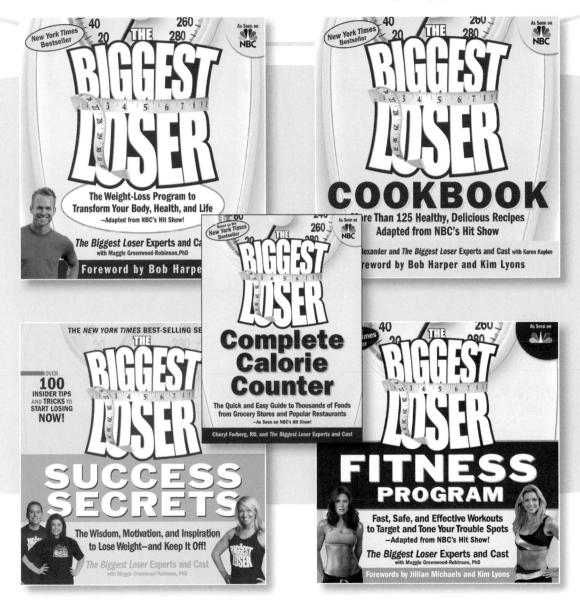

Available wherever books are sold.

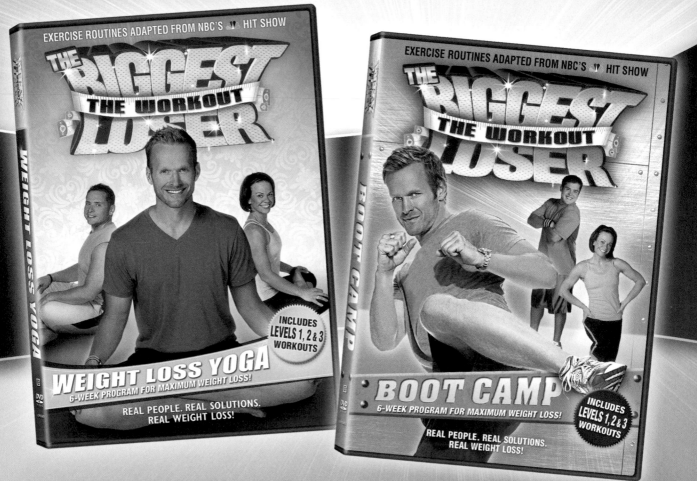